Secret Places of West Dorset

Some reviews

'It goes off the beaten track to cover folklore, curiosities, legends and history as well as churches, ancient trackways and enigmatic stones.'

Bridport News

'This little gem of a book demonstrates just how much there is to be discovered west of Weymouth. ... Some of these places are atmospheric simply because they are wild and empty; others have faint traces of some lost and mysterious past. Well written and informative, the book is beautifully illustrated with colour photographs and the author's watercolours.'

Steve Marshall, *Fortean Times*

'*Secret Places of West Dorset* elegantly invites us to explore this magical and at times transcendental area. The book achieves a literary feel without ever being difficult or a chore to read. The writing feels very free, moulding personal experiences with literary, historical and folk references.'

Dorset Echo

'Even if you don't go out to enjoy the suggested walks, you can cosy up in your armchair and explore in your mind Dorset's folklore, curiosities, legends and history. ... The many photographs and author's own paintings help to illustrate the rare beauty of this part of the county.'

Dark Dorset

The Hell Stone above Portesham.

More Secret Places of West Dorset

Louise Hodgson

Roving Press

Published by Roving Press Ltd
4 Southover Cottages, Frampton, Dorset, DT2 9NQ, UK
Tel: +44 (0)1300 321531
www.rovingpress.co.uk

First published 2016 by Roving Press Ltd

ISBN: 978-1-906651-282

British Library Cataloguing in Publication Data
A catalogue record for this book is available from the British Library

Artwork by Louise Hodgson
Photographs by Roving Press and Louise Hodgson
Map and cover design by Roving Press

Front cover photograph: the garderobe at Wolfeton House.

Set in 11.5/13 pt Minion by Beamreach Printing (www.beamreachuk.co.uk)
Printed and bound by Henry Ling Ltd., at the Dorset Press, Dorchester, DT1 1HD.

Contents

Acknowledgements

Many thanks to Tim and Julie Musk for their hard work in compiling a book from the morass of my writings. I have also been encouraged by the wonderful responses by many readers to my first book *Secret Places of West Dorset* which has spawned this further volume of explorations.

How to Use This Book

Places appear alphabetically for ease of location, with clear directions to get you there by car/bike, including Ordnance Survey map number and grid references. Many places have limited access, so please be respectful when parking your car and visiting. Some of the locations are one-off places to visit and enjoy, others have ideas for stimulating walks, and it is possible to link many of them to enjoy a full day out. It is essential to carry the appropriate OS map for the area so you can devise walks to suit your abilities.

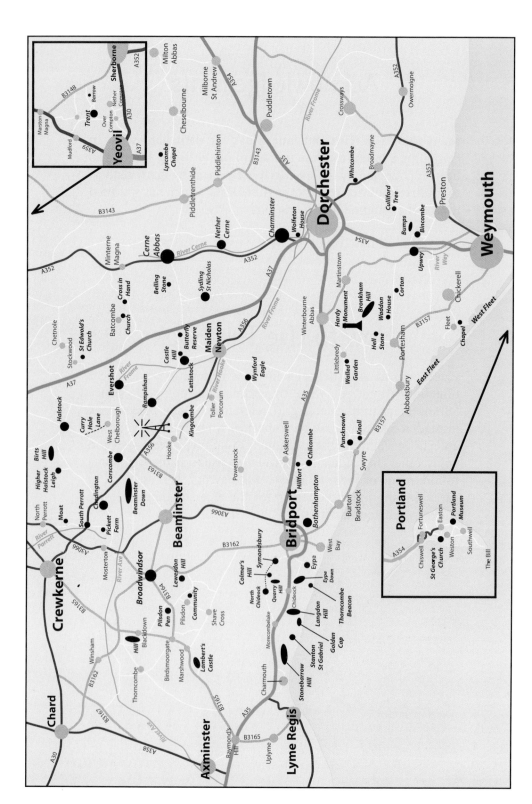

Introduction

Since my first book, *Secret Places of West Dorset*, was published, I've always felt there was more to discover in this part of the county; more mysterious, atmospheric and provocative places that stimulate our powers of imagination and heighten our ability to empathise with the natural landscape. The drive to explore is within most us to varying degrees and West Dorset is one of those places where exploration can easily lead to adventures beyond the usual and ordinary.

The landscape in this area of England is mainly that of valley and hill, with a variety of woodland – beech, oak and ash predominating. A proportion of the hills are wooded but the majority are bare, with distinctive wind-carved shapes. This varied landscape acts on the senses in many ways.

The reasons why some countryside experiences are more memorable than others are myriad. Sometimes they can be triggered by a special sense of 'place', difficult to describe but felt in a visceral way. Sometimes the reasons are more obvious, such as an uplifting view, stormy sea, ancient paths and unspoilt woodland, the sort of scenery in which West Dorset excels.

Some of the descriptive village names, such as Melbury Bubb, Rhyme Intrinseca, Toller Porcorum, Whitchurch Canonicorum and Wynford Eagle not only are redolent of history and place but also seem touched by a medley of languages – Latin, Anglo-Saxon, Norse and Gaelic – echoing past invasions.

Folk beliefs that have a geographical reality and focus can embed themselves in the landscape and memory. In older times the land was seen as alive and vibrant with the flow of natural forces, something recognised by the Chinese and exemplified by their art of *feng shui*. Some areas seem to have a concentration of energy and these could be seen as sacred places. Often they were specific landscape features, such as rocky outcrops, a certain hill, caves, springs and trees and areas of woodland. Sometimes these places were marked by standing stones, henges or dolmens. When an area or landscape feature has linked with it a legend bringing in the Otherworldly or more outré aspect of the countryside, it develops a deeper significance. Some places are said to offer entrances to the Underworld, allowing for communication between different levels of reality. For example, the tale of the pool at Trent, near Sherborne, with its connotations of King Arthur and ghostly happenings, excites not only a physical appreciation but also an imaginative one.

When a place has folklore associations, the more curious individual might wonder why; why here and not another place? Some locations seem to have, by their very nature, a fine balance and presence. There are also landscapes that are linked with a family. In ancient times old families often had a symbiotic relationship with the lands they owned. The Scottish clans, for example, exemplify this kinship with the land, as represented by their plaids, heraldic emblems and history and legends. These families share a blood relationship with the land and their links go very deep.

In writing this book, I highlight some memorable special places that are not particularly well known. I hope that the interest and pleasure these countryside explorations bring will harness a curiosity and appreciation of the landscape and our role therein. Many of the places mentioned are a product of natural features linked with human influences in an area, one example being the vast flocks of sheep that grazed the downland of Dorset, close-cropping the herbage to produce the swathes of grassland that can still be seen, rolling and rippling through near and far distances.

Those who live in West Dorset are fortunate, and those who visit, appreciative. This part of the county has in its diversity a store of delights. One found treasure inexorably leads to another. The spirit of enquiry can be dampened by the easy informational excesses of computer and mobile telephone. If those machines are put aside and one puts on walking boots, pockets a map, opens the door and strides out, then another, different reality manifests, one that is lived and breathed and has nuance and meaning.

BATCOMBE
'Conjuring Minterne' and a Wayside Pillar

OS maps: Explorer 117 or Landranger 194

Grid refs: Hilfield Hill Nature Reserve ST557872, Church ST556878

Directions: From the A37 Yeovil to Dorchester road, take the turning to Batcombe opposite the Evershot turn-off. This small road is called Haydon Lane; keep right for Batcombe Hill. After approx. 2 miles and before the woods, the pillar is set into the wire fence-line on your left. Park further on at Hilfield Hill Nature Reserve (the entrance is narrow but it is safer than parking on the lane). Walk back to the pillar. To visit the church, drive back past the pillar, to the narrow, steep and winding Stile Way on the right, signed Batcombe. At the bottom of the hill is the church, which has a grassy car park.

The name Batcombe brings to mind a small hidden valley, haunted by the night-time flutter of bats. The truth is that there are no more bats here than anywhere else in the vicinity and the 'combe' is above the village, being part of the precipitous lane that leads down into the community from the hills above. Batcombe lies in the lee of the chalk downs and is an old settlement with an interesting history.

The view northwards from Batcombe Down.

3

The local squires used to be the Minternes, who have given their name to various villages in the area. One of their number, John, was infamous for, amongst other strange deeds, supposedly forcing his horse to jump over the church. John Minterne or 'Conjuring Minterne' was known as a cunning man or sorcerer and a practitioner of the magical arts. Whether he favoured the academic over the active magical practices is not known, nor has any written evidence of his studies come to light, but his local notoriety was probably worthy of a large degree of justification.

St Mary Magdalene Church, Batcombe, sitting in the lee of the downs.

The occasion of his above-mentioned massive leap over the church was caused by his sudden remembrance that he had left a book of magical writings open on his table. This wasn't a tome that would be easy reading to the casual eye, and so, mindful of the fear it could provoke amongst family or servants, he made haste to return to his manor. Legend has it that with supernatural confidence, and a bit of help from the Devil, he galloped over the hill behind the church and spurred his horse to perform the stupendous leap over the church, landing just beyond the graveyard. It is said that grass will not grow on that spot, known as the Pitching Plot. Both rider and horse survived the leap, but the church was slighted by the horse's hooves which knocked off one of the four pinnacles gracing the tower.

There are two main contenders for John 'Conjuring Minterne'. The Minternes were a well-known Dorset family who had connections with the courts of Henry VIII and Elizabeth I. There was a John Minterne who studied at Oxford, was a member of Elizabeth's Privy Council and who lived between 1514 and 1592.

He had a son, also called John, who lived between 1540 and 1681. The author feels that the earlier John was the 'Conjuring Minterne'. Queen Elizabeth I had Dr John Dee, an astrologer, alchemist and magician, resident in her court and was thus not adverse to those of a magical persuasion.

Prior to intensive changes to the church, carried out by John Hicks in 1864, there used to be a chapel attached to the main building. This chapel was the Minterne family chapel and was largely destroyed during the church's restoration. Some of the family memorial tablets have been repositioned on the north side of the tower, but many have now gone. Conjuring Minterne's request was to be buried half in half out of the church, and, if his demand was met, it would be in the family chapel that half of him would have been buried, with the other half in the graveyard beyond the church wall. His ivy-clad stone chest tomb can be seen near the porch, overgrown and neglected. There is an inscription on the left wall just inside the church door to John Minterne 1592. There is also an inscription to another John Minterne dated 1705.

The church is built on the site of an early 11th-century church. The current building is now redundant but is normally unlocked. The tower is 15th century and the font is constructed with a column of hamstone dating from Norman times, with an earlier Saxon limestone cuboid basin.

No-one really knows the origin or history of this mysterious wayside pillar, known locally as the Cross and Hand.

From the 16th through to the 18th century, Minterne manor house was a fine edifice in the centre of the village on Wriggle River Lane. The situation remains unchanged, although some of the surrounding buildings have now gone. The house is currently known as Newlands Farm but has been rebuilt over the years. It retains a vestige of its former glory in the 17th-century arch over the garden gate, which is inscribed with the date 1622.

Above Batcombe Down, on land that used to be wild heath, is another conundrum, a small wayside pillar known as the Cross and Hand, which is Grade II listed and a Scheduled Ancient Monument. Offerings of coins are sometimes made here. There used to be an inn in Batcombe named the Cross in Hand, but it closed years ago. The naming of this pillar is intriguing as it is difficult to discern any hand or cross; maybe the term is not to be taken literally but as something that pilgrims should be clutching – a small cross in their hands; this could be for one of two reasons: this was a holy place and should be visited with the true regard for a wayside shrine, or it was haunted and one should have a cross in one's hand to ward off apparitions.

The rounded shape is reminiscent of a type of mediaeval Mercian cross mainly found in the Midlands and north of England. A broken example known as the Pillar of Eliseg stands near Valle Crucis Abbey, just outside Llangollen in North Wales. It was erected by a king of Powys, Cyngen ap Cadell, in the 9th century to commemorate his great-grandfather, Elisedd ap Gwylog, a great warrior king who reclaimed Powys after it had been semi-colonised by the English. The pillar was damaged by the Roundheads during the Civil War and regrettably the lower half has disappeared. The inscription on the remaining top half was copied in 1696 which saved the text, as the original is now so worn as to be illegible.

It is hard to fix an age to the stone pillar above Batcombe. It has been mooted as being Roman, Saxon or possibly Norman. There are various stories attached to it. One suggests it could have been a preaching cross, another that it marks the grave of a murderer, who was executed here where he committed the crime, and his ghost haunts this place. Perhaps it is the parish boundary. Or the spot where, in the Dark Ages, four local kings made their peace and promised a cessation of skirmish. There is also the tale, expounded by Thomas Hardy, of the lost pyx, perhaps the most colourful legend of all; and in Hardy's novel *Tess of the D'Urbervilles*, Alec asks Tess to swear on the pillar that she will never tempt him by her charms and ways. She later asks a shepherd the meaning of the Cross and Hand and he says it is no holy place but a medieval torture device and place of ill omen.

Hendover Coppice Reserve is particularly worth visiting in spring when the bluebells are in flower, and an added bonus is that dormice have been seen here.

There is a barely discernible tumulus in the field by the pillar and the prehistoric Wessex Ridgeway passes 500 m south-east of here. Also nearby is the ancient Roman road (now the A37) travelling from Ilchester in Somerset to the Roman stronghold of Dorchester.

The Dorset Wildlife Trust owns a piece of steeply sloping woodland called Hendover Coppice Reserve about 300 m up the road, just west of the minor road that leads down to the Friary of St Francis at Hilfield. This peaceful wooded site of 30 acres (12 ha) was probably once used as a place for reflection by the friars.

The Lost Pyx: A Mediaeval Legend
by Thomas Hardy

Some say the spot is banned; that the pillar Cross-and-Hand
Attests to a deed of hell;
But of else than of bale is the mystic tale
That ancient Vale-folk tell.

Ere Cernel's Abbey ceased hereabout there dwelt a priest,
(In later life sub-prior
Of the brotherhood there, whose bones are now bare
In the field that was Cernel choir).

One night in his cell at the foot of yon dell
The priest heard a frequent cry:
'Go, father, in haste to the cot on the waste,
And shrive a man waiting to die.'

Said the priest in a shout to the caller without,
'The night howls, the tree-trunks bow;
One may barely by day track so rugged a way,
And can I then do so now?'

No further word from the dark was heard,
And the priest moved never a limb;
And he slept and dreamed; till a Visage seemed
To frown from Heaven at him.

In a sweat he arose; and the storm shrieked shrill,
And smote as in savage joy;
While High-Stoy trees twanged to Bubb-Down Hill,
And Bubb-Down to High-Stoy.

There seemed not a holy thing in hail,
Nor shape of light or love,
From the Abbey north of Blackmore Vale
To the Abbey south thereof.

Yet he plodded thence through the dark immense,
And with many a stumbling stride
Through copse and briar climbed nigh and nigher
To the cot and the sick man's side.

When he would have unslung the Vessels uphung
To his arm in the steep ascent,
He made loud moan: the Pyx was gone
Of the Blessed Sacrament.

Then in dolorous dread he beat his head:
'No earthly prize or pelf
Is the thing I've lost in tempest tossed,
But the Body of Christ Himself!'

He thought of the Visage his dream revealed,
And turned towards whence he came,
Hands groping the ground along foot-track and field,
And head in a heat of shame.

Till here on the hill, betwixt vill and vill,
He noted a clear straight ray
Stretching down from the sky to a spot hard by,
Which shone with the light of day.

And gathered around the illumined ground
Were common beasts and rare,
All kneeling at gaze, and in pause profound
Attent on an object there.

'Twas the Pyx, unharmed 'mid the circling rows
Of Blackmore's hairy throng,
Whereof were oxen, sheep, and does,
And hares from the brakes among;

And badgers grey, and conies keen,
And squirrels of the tree,
And many a member seldom seen
Of Nature's family.

The ireful winds that scoured and swept
Through coppice, clump, and dell,
Within that holy circle slept
Calm as in hermit's cell.

Then the priest bent likewise to the sod
And thanked the Lord of Love,
And Blessed Mary, Mother of God,
And all the saints above.

And turning straight with his priceless freight,
He reached the dying one,
Whose passing sprite had been stayed for the rite
Without which bliss hath none.

And when by grace the priest won place,
And served the Abbey well,
He reared this stone to mark where shone
That midnight miracle.

BEAMINSTER DOWN
An Old Drove and Lone Oak Tree

OS maps: Explorer 117 or Landranger 194

Grid ref: Parking along track ST496034

Directions: From Beaminster take the A3066 north-east towards Mosterton for approx. 1.5 miles. Immediately after the tunnel, turn sharp right, signed Maiden Newton. Follow this road along the ridge for 1.5 miles until a track on your left to East Axnoller Farm. Take the track until you see a small tree in the field on the left near a meeting of paths and gates, then park appropriately. You may have noticed the obvious tumulus in the field on the right at the start of the track. To see the more hidden tumulus, having parked, proceed a short distance down the track on foot, and after passing through the hedge line, take the right path for a few hundred metres. There is a scrubby wood on the right with the tumulus beyond.

Beaminster Down lies about a mile or so east of Beaminster and is a swathe of chalk downland rising above the small town. This area of land is fairly extensively farmed, although there are some fields that have escaped the incursion of the plough. East Axnoller Farm, which encompasses much of the land, consists of 148 acres. It was bought by the Donkey Sanctuary near Sidmouth in 1990 for grazing some of their rescued donkeys and making haylage and is one of seven farms owned by the charity. Sheep also graze this grassy downland, to complement the donkeys when it is too wet for them to be outside.

This is an historical area. Some standing stones, the Hore Stones, lie prone and hidden in a swathe of brambles within a grassy triangle between two roads, the A356 and road to Beaminster. At the top of the down, near a crossroads,

Rescued donkeys in fields on Beaminster Down.

leading on the one hand to Maiden Newton and the other towards the A3066, there is a tumulus, which is clearly visible. However, not many people are aware that there is another, out of view and somewhat hidden, in a far corner of the same field. It has not totally survived the encroaching badger setts or human disturbance over the years, yet is still recognisably a tumulus, an ostensibly plain, earthen mound, which has survived here for thousands of years. Prehistoric ritual and religious structures will forever be an enigma for us, as this period of our history dates from so long ago, when life was utterly different from the modernity of today. These tumuli date from the Bronze Age, a time when many stone circles were also erected. Stone circles in particular capture the imagination, because no one quite knows their true usage or purpose. Links with astrological formations, the seasons, position of the sun, rites of death and rites of life are all posited as explanations.

A tumulus on the downs.

Tumuli obviously had a different purpose: primarily as a memorial to the dead and possibly as a tribal marker. Many tumuli were built on the skyline, where they can be seen from afar, marking identity and perhaps acting in a guardian capacity. If a tumulus contained the remains of a warrior, it could be construed that the warrior, on some level, still had the capacity to protect the tribe, if not from physical harm, at least from supernatural attack. Looking at tribes exant today, who have a way of life probably similar to our early ancestors, such as the New Guinea people, it can be seen how much the supernatural world affects their lives.

The world of prehistory is one where there is an inner vibrancy behind the seemingly mundane. A tree, for example, is seen as being peopled by an entity that carries the identity of the tree as a sort of codified template; that is, the outer shape – its trunk, branches, leaves, etc. – does not necessarily show us the full picture. Tolkien hints at this with his 'Ents', trees that walked and who had formidable power. Tribespeople who have not been beguiled by television and other aspects of the modern world would, and still do, in similarity to our prehistoric ancestors, believe in the spirits that inhabit living things. These spirits aren't subject to death, as we know it, and here we return to our dead warrior. His spirit wouldn't be 'trapped' in the vicinity of the place where he was buried. His spirit and soul would have gone on to the timeless zone that is beyond physical existence. However, there would be an aspect of the archetypal 'warrior' that would still perform its purpose, that of protecting the tribespeople.

When, over the years, the tribe, for various reasons, dispersed, possibly the old mound was dug. What was there was scattered, or placed in some drawer in a museum, and what few relics that remained, perhaps overlooked, would not have been enough to hold any more than the faintest trace of what had been. The old tumulus would become the shell of an ancient memory, lost to the winds and empty.

Ancient trackways often run close to tumuli and this area is no exception. Close by the second tumulus and marked by a footpath sign is a track, part of an ancient ridgeway which travels across the downs and the main road to Dorchester. This is a route that would have been taken by drovers moving livestock to market. In the 18th century, there were around 600,000 sheep within a 6-mile radius of Dorchester. Old droves where animals were driven to fresh grazing or market still exist, for instance at Broadmayne where the names Bramble Drove and South Drove can be found. 'Ridgeway' is a generic term describing a particular type of ancient road that travels across the hard chalk surfaces of hilltop ridges and it distinguishes a high travel route from a low one. The thin soil and rocky chalky subsoil need very little maintenance and a trail is formed, caused by footfall, driven domestic animal movement and wheeled carts and other vehicles. Ridgeways are a typical feature of long-distance routes, only descending to cross valleys and the occasional water-course.

The Romans adopted some of the ridgeway routes, appreciating the fact that, apart from inheriting a ready-made road, albeit rough in places, they would be travelling, in the main, across open country, where the road would give good views of any possible marauders or rival armed factions. The element of surprise, so important in many battles, would be almost entirely absent in these upland airy spaces.

The joys to be found in walking these ancient trackways comprise a mixture of many things, from the peace and spacious views to the multitude of wildflowers that thrive here. Cow-parsley, purple knapweed and Queen Anne's lace are a few amongst many plants that grow alongside old tracks on the chalk downland.

The trackway here, affording fine views in parts, is somehow atmospheric. There is a bucolic quality, maybe left over from it being an ancient drovers' route. It is the sort of track that delights with a certain simplicity, as the way leads through varying countryside. Here, one's sense of appreciation is heightened by a feeling of kinship with the past. We are lucky that in Britain we still have many of these old ways, a legacy from prehistoric times. They are the arteries of the land, allowing for movement of many differing kinds and giving free access to areas of subtle beauty and historical importance. Access to many of our ancient historical sites is afforded by these tracks, as here, passing near to two tumuli.

Back at the farm track, there is a small oak tree in the field to the west. The field has been cleared of all trees and bushes over the years and is now regularly ploughed and planted. This hill field is rather featureless apart from this wind-shaped oak. Why this one tree has been left is intriguing. Local people have said that, for them, this tree has a quality that is difficult to describe other than a sort of fae benevolence. It bears the marks of a fairy tree.

A lone oak, weathering time.

To give it the nomenclature of 'fairy tree' might seem overly imaginative, but in the old days fairy trees were part of the landscape and treated with care. England has lost most of them now, but there is still a tradition and veneration of sacred trees in Ireland. For example, at the foot of the fairy hillfort Lios Ard, near the village of Kiltimagh in County Mayo, is an ancient spreading oak where at certain times it is said is heard the strange lilt of fairy music, as the fae are said to dance around the tree.

The fairy hawthorn is a tree that brings ill-luck to those foolhardy enough to cut it down. What marks out a fairy thorn from other thorn trees is that it stands alone, as do all fairy trees. These trees could be in the middle of a field or by a crossroads, at the edge of a wood or beside a holy well (with which they are often associated). Sometimes rags are tied to the branches, where these trees are known as 'wishing trees' and people's wishes are exemplified by the rags.

Apart from hawthorn, the other fairy trees are oak and ash, and these are also known as the three main Celtic sacred trees. The hawthorn is the tree between worlds and is associated with May ceremonies, oak is guardian, while ash was used for spears and ships. Until the 20th century, it was considered unlucky to use the term 'fairy tree' and they were instead known as a 'lone tree' or sometimes 'gentry tree' and were largely left alone. Seen as portals to the fairy realm, a sort of parallel world to ours, where the reality and rules are different, these trees are both firmly physical but also 'other'. They can act as way-showers to a different realm, where no rules that we can recognise exist and where vision has a different truth.

In this particular area of countryside, a couple of miles out of Beaminster, are found three iconic features in the landscape – a special tree, subtly situated tumulus and prehistoric trackway. These features are not obvious; they have to be sought out. Together they illustrate some of the mysteries of the landscape.

BINCOMBE
Bincombe Bumps and Culliford Tree

OS maps: Explorer OL15 or Landranger 194

Grid refs: Bincombe roadside parking SY686846, Culliford Tree SY699854

Directions: Bincombe, on the northern outskirts of Weymouth, can be accessed by turning off the A354 Dorchester to Weymouth road. Bincombe Hill, where the tumuli are situated, is above and to the north of the village, reached by a trackway which starts near the church. There are fine views from this high point over Weymouth and Portland Harbour, Chalbury Camp hillfort to the east, and the Culliford Tree and numerous tumuli to the north. For the Culliford Tree, drive south out of Bincombe, then east on the A353 above Littlemoor. Take the first left in Preston, Coombe Valley Road. Proceed uphill for approx. 2 miles, ignore the right turn to Sutton Poyntz and further on at the crossroads the Culliford Tree is in the field ahead.
There is verge/layby parking to the left.

'Bincombe' derives from the Saxon meaning a 'valley where beans grow'. Some place names around ridgeway tracks are over a thousand years old and are British names, predating the Roman period. Bincombe is a small village a few miles north of Weymouth, yet despite proximity to such a large and busy town, it has a remote feel and appears little visited. It lies in the lee of Bincombe Hill, which rises steeply and provides a pastoral backdrop to the settlement below. Archaeologists have found flint tools dating from Neolithic times (500,000 BC)

A village at the foot of the downs.

The steep path up to 'Bincombe Bumps'. From around here allegedly, the Grand Old Duke of York marched his 10,000 men to the top – and yes, he marched them down again!

on its slopes and a later Bronze Age collection of flint and bone artefacts and shards of pottery in the area.

Burial methods between these two cultures differed: whereas mass burials, perhaps members of the same family, are found in the long barrows of the Neolithic, in later times individuals were buried in single graves, marked by mounds of earth – known as a tumulus or barrow (see preceding chapter). A barrow is basically a round or oblong mound, often with a ditch around it, and it would have originally been white, because they are mainly found on chalk. The body was placed on its side in a crouched position and normally surrounded by grave goods, such as clay beakers and arrowheads and articles of personal ornamentation. Later, bodies were cremated and the remains buried in urns.

Over 2000 barrows are known in Dorset, with a large concentration along the South Dorset Ridgeway, the most famous of the prehistoric roads that criss-cross the chalk hills of south-western England. Many can still be seen in the Bincombe area and go by the name of 'Bincombe Bumps'. Others appear as crop marks, faintly scouring the fields.

'Marys' is the old Dorset dialect name for barrows such as these above Bincombe.

In the early barrows, a beaker was often placed with the body. The Clandon Barrow, 3 miles to the north-east at Martinstown, which was dug in 1882, revealed a bronze dagger, polished stone mace head, amber cup and golden-decorated lozenge-shaped item. The stone for the mace head came from Highland Britain, amber from Scandinavia and gold from Wales or Ireland. The person whose grave this was must have been hugely important to the tribe to warrant such valuable grave goods.

Barrows continued to be built for around 2000 years, with some re-used periodically over the centuries. There is evidence that a number were later conserved as markers for the positioning of Celtic fields. Barrows are associated with tribes of immigrants from the Rhineland area of mainland Europe known as the Beaker people (because of the clay vessels found in their graves). These people, along with earlier Neolithic folk, are also connected with certain henges and early Bronze Age standing stones.

There are various forms of round barrow, with the *bowl* barrow being the most common. The *bell* barrow has a platform between the mound and surrounding ditch. The *disk* barrow has a smaller mound surrounded by a ditch and high outer bank. The rarer *pond* barrow is a rounded depression within a low bank. The rarer still *saucer* barrow has a low mound and ditch but no bank.

Later barrows contained a primary centrally located burial, sometimes with other burials, thought to date from the same time, placed within the mound or in the surrounding ditch. Secondary burials of a later date have been found, and sometimes the mounds were used for burials in the Iron Age and even into Roman and Saxon times. Cremated remains, placed inside a large pottery urn, became a feature from the Mid-Bronze Age onwards and have also been found in earlier barrows.

Some barrows have legendary status. The Culliford Tree, also known as the Music Barrow, is 1 mile north-east, near Came Wood, 'a wood belonging to the Abbey of Caen', on the hill above Bincombe alongside a small lane that leads to Broadmayne. It is reputed that fairy music has been heard coming forth from the barrow and also a voice issuing advice. A woman who was planning to build a house in close vicinity of this earthwork heard a voice as if coming from the tops of the trees on the barrow. She was so frightened by this that she decided not to build her house anywhere in the area. Apparently, the way to hear the fairy music is to press your ear to the centre of the barrow at mid-day. Fairies have historically been associated with certain mounds and barrows in Britain, and also treasure is linked to various mounds but seldom, if ever, found.

In the 19th century, excavation of the Culliford Tree barrow revealed four burials towards the surface of the mound. A necklace of amber beads, two of which were clasped with gold, was found with a female skeleton. These remains were thought to be Saxon and were secondary burials in a much earlier burial mound. Culliford Tree was also used as a Saxon meeting place of the 'hundred court'. A 'hundred' was a group of estates linked together for legal and administrative purposes. Principal meetings or 'moots' were held twice-yearly at a prearranged site. There were approximately 39 hundreds in Mediaeval Dorset and these were devised in the 10th century, prior to the Norman invasion. With the advent of Norman administration, these 'hundreds' gradually died out.

For many years, the barrow was a traditional gypsy camp ground, and for a few months the travellers would make their home here, on the sweeping downland. In the evenings they would loose their long-legged lurchers to begin the savage ballet of the chase, the outcome of which would wind up gently simmering in a pot atop an open fire.

View from Bincombe Bumps of Came Down Wood and the Culliford Tree barrow.

This large barrow has a grim history, for during the Monmouth Rebellion of 1685, Judge Jefferies, ensconced for a while in Dorchester, was doling out punishments of cruel barbarity. On this barrow, body parts from those of Monmouth's army, the poor souls who had been caught and had ended up with the cruellest of fates, that of being hung, drawn and quartered, were displayed on its banks. 'Burning Barrow' is another bowl barrow situated on the Ridgeway above Bincombe and south of Culliford Tree. It gained its name because it has a reputation for sometimes showing an orange glow around its top. Apparently, in the early 1980s, a woman was riding pillion on a motorbike and saw this strange occurrence, complete with reddish projections that looked like flames.

There is a long barrow on Bincombe Hill a few hundred metres north of the Bumps, beside a drystone wall. It was possibly the precursor to the Bincombe Hill group of round barrows. In 1922 a large bowl barrow was excavated, with the whole barrow being removed. The inside of the mound was lined with stone. Eight skeletons, including that of a 6-month-old baby, were found. Two of the skeletons were in stone cists and four had pots accompanying them.

During the Napoleonic Wars (1793–1815), a legion from the York Hussars was camped on Bincombe Hill. Two young soldiers deserted but were hunted down and summarily shot. Their remains lie in an unmarked grave in Bincombe churchyard. The church is dedicated to the Holy Trinity. The chancel and nave date from the 12th century, with some rebuilding during the 15th and 19th centuries. The whole church was extensively restored in 1862.

The area in and around Bincombe carries the template of our early history; thousands of years have passed, yet many of these simple prehistoric records of our early ancestors still remain here, to be valued as intriguing memories of our past.

The slopes of Bincombe Down.

BLACKDOWN
A Forgotten Hill

OS maps: Explorer 116 or Landranger 193

Grid refs: Venn Chapel ST390040, Cole's Cross ST396025

Directions: Blackdown is situated on the B3165, approx. mid-way between Crewkerne and the A35 at Raymond's Hill. The B3165 is a busy road with little parking, so the hill is best accessed from Causeway Lane which runs the length of the hill, to the west. Park respectfully between Venn Chapel (north) and Cole's Cross (south). There are three paths up the hill. It may also be possible to park at Blackdown Village Hall just south of Cole's Cross.

The Wessex Ridgeway runs for approximately 62 miles from Cranborne Chase to Lyme Regis. It forms part of the great Ridgeway, a prehistoric trade and travelling route that stretches across Britain, linking the Norfolk and Devon coasts. Before reaching Blackdown, the Ridgeway passes over the hillfort of Lambert's Castle and flanks of Pilsdon Pen. After Pilsdon, the way travels the length of Blackdown Hill ridge for 1.5 miles.

Blackdown Hill, which rises to 215 m.

Another long-distance path, the Jubilee Trail, passes through Cole's Cross. This path was established to celebrate the 60th anniversary of the founding of the Ramblers Association and runs from Forde Abbey on the Somerset border to Bokerley Dyke on the Hampshire border, seeking out little known paths along its 88-mile length.

The view north.

Blackdown is part of the parish of Kittwhistle, a strangely named village situated on the north-east side of the hill. Although the better known Blackdown Hills that range across parts of east Devon and west Somerset are largely what are brought to mind with the word 'Blackdown', this smallish hill/ridge has its own identity and is worth exploring. Blackdown's more showy neighbours, Pilsdon Pen, Lambert's Castle and Coney's Castle, seem to be far more popular with walkers, yet, to my mind, Blackdown has as great a beauty and variety. There are wildflower meadows, grassy hillsides where butterflies, including Blues, flutter in the sun, areas of gorse bushes, pastureland, trees – both singly and in clumps – and beyond them views of Somerset, Dorset and Devon. The footpaths on this hill look barely used, partly because there is no clearly defined parking for visitors.

Meadow flowers on the slopes of Blackdown.

The atmosphere on Blackdown can be inspiring; the hill feels as if it were a secret waiting to be discovered. A small stream called Temple Brook originates between Blackdown and Pilsdon Pen, to the south-west. It is an interesting name for a stream and where it rises is a strange lost area of raggedy fields and twisted trees. It is an 'in-between' place, an area of liminality. 'Back country' is a term for an area with an aura of unapproachability; this can come from both the setting and something else, something subtle and unprincipled. In some places, such as this area of Blackdown, there is the feeling of a piece of land touched by wilderness.

The land, vegetation and wildlife here have been left to their own devices.

Although the hill is one of the more modest in the area, the view from Blackdown has a particular intimacy that some of the higher vantage points lack. Blackdown is lovely and harbours the whispered subtlety that can still be found in certain places of the British Isles. These are the areas where the message has to be sought by an understanding of nuance. It is here that discernment is rewarded by quiet revelation – the revelation afforded to poets and philosophers, yet also available for all.

BOTHENHAMPTON
An Historic Church and Downland

OS maps: Explorer 116 or OL15, or Landranger 193

Grid refs: Bothenhampton roadside parking SY474918

Directions: From the main roundabout at the southern end of Bridport (by Groves Nursery), take the A35 north for just 300 m and turn right to Bothenhampton. This is aptly named Hollow Way, which rises gradually and has an extensive raised pavement. Continue past the 'new' church, then after a further 200 m bear left up Old Church Road. Park before the road veers sharply right, and walk up to the historic church. To access the ridge north of the church, walk back down the track and take the steep footpath opposite the Old School or further on the bridleway, which is slightly easier. From the bottom of Old Church Lane, a pleasant walk for the downland to the south is to take Quarry Lane opposite, through the Nature Reserve and up the wooded hillside.

The simple interior of Holy Trinity old church contains an elegantly designed Georgian reredos with sturdy communion rails.

Holy Trinity old church exists as a 13th-century chancel and a 15th-century tower. The rest of the church was demolished in the 1880s due to general dereliction. It was also thought by the parishioners that the old church was too small to serve the local community, and a new church was built in the Arts and Craft style at the other end of the village. The old church was used as a mortuary chapel for some years, but in 1971, due to increasing instability of the remaining structure, it was declared redundant and in the following year became the responsibility of the Churches Conservation Trust.

Positioned here, at the end of a lane and under the lea of the downs, there is a feeling of bucolic pastoral tranquillity. For generations this church has served the country people of the area – the farm-workers, hedgers and ditchers, blacksmiths and other folk who lived in and around the village. Their graves are scattered in the churchyard and through the headstones their names live on, even if the families have long gone.

The village of Bothenhampton now extends beyond the cottages that are strung along the main street with its attractive raised footpath. There is an old farm situated down a side road, Duck Street, and some pretty cottages, but the main attraction to Bothenhampton is perhaps its setting below the downs.

The high ridge immediately to the north affords panoramic views of West Bay, Bridport and Walditch. Going east along the ridge takes you to Shipton Gorge.

Bridleway leading to the downs north of the church.

View over Bridport and beyond.

The path to the downs south of the village passes through Wanderwell Quarry, now a nature reserve. The quarried stone here is known as Forest Marble and was used in the walls and foundations of local buildings from the 14th century up until the 1930s, when the quarry closed. The historical value of the area is recognised by Dorset's Important Geological Sites Group (DIGS) and by it being classed as a Regionally Important Geological/Geomorphological Site (RIGS).

Bothenhampton Local Nature Reserve.

The downs to the south have been pastureland for hundreds of years, and the original cover of gorse, bracken, shrubs and trees has largely been cleared, affording a vista that serves as a tonic for the senses. In every direction there are far-reaching views: in the south, the luminous glistening of the sea; to the west, iconic Colmer's Hill, coupled with the distant bulks of Pilsdon Pen and Lewesdon Hill; and in the further distance, the rolling hills of Devon.

Chalk downland spreads over southern England, giving West Dorset its rolling hills. Within the folds and on the heights and slopes are some mysterious and beautiful places which are seldom visited. When people come to Dorset, they are invariably drawn to the coast or to ancient ruins such as Corfe Castle and perhaps to the various historic buildings that are found in the county. Apart from a few ramblers, the downland interior is largely overlooked and it is left to the farmers and locals to appreciate its subtle beauties. Although large areas have been turned by the plough and the hilltops hold few trees, there is enough left of pasture and scrub to convey the essence of what this type of landscape has to offer.

The downland of the southern counties of Britain has always provided some wonderful vantage points. Ancient trackways, some as early as Neolithic, run along the crests of the hills and offer a good sight-line, ensuring that enemies coming by land or sea could be seen from a long way off and precautions swiftly put in place. Many of the prehistoric hillforts of these early times still exist as earthworks, with their residual banks and ditches.

To the artist's eye, white chalk and pale grasses reflect and hold light, and even on a dark day the downs give the walker a sense of this quality. The land also comes with another sense, that of nature's immensity. This is reflected in the rolling bulk of the hills as they spread out in waves. Walking on the hills above Bothenhampton, with the strong sense of the nearby sea and feeling the soft, sheep-cropped turf underfoot, one senses a little-changed, timeless atmosphere. Enough remains to remind one of the old days when the shepherds summered here with their flocks, and sheep were one of the main sources of wealth for the Dorset farmer.

BROADWINDSOR
A Venerable Yew

OS maps: Explorer 116 or Landranger 193

Grid refs: Broadwindsor roadside parking and Church ST437026

Directions: Broadwindsor is approx. 7 miles north of Bridport on the B3162, or 2 miles west of Beaminster on the B3163. There is generally plenty of on-road parking in the village. The church can be approached on foot from the south or east.

Broadwindsor is set in a hill-strewn landscape of indolent charm and character. As in practically every village in Dorset, this settlement is a mix of old houses and new. The church, set on a hill, dominates the village, and the immediate area of the church is one of the more attractive parts of this small community.

King Charles II hid in the village for a night during his flight from Cromwell and his troops after the Battle of Worcester. The date was 23 September 1651 and this is commemorated with a plaque on the cottage next to the Old George Inn. Charles was a wanted man and a reward of £1000, an enormous sum in those days, was offered to whoever captured the King. Had Charles been caught, he and anyone aiding him would have been executed for treason. The fact that the King was unusual looking, of swarthy complexion and over 6 ft tall made escape hugely problematic. Charles managed to discretely travel from Bridport to Broadwindsor, where he was hidden in the George Inn, owned by Rhys Jones, presumably a Welshman. Charles, with a few supporters, was given rooms on the top floor. Later in the night the local constable turned up with around 40 soldiers, all wanting billets in the inn. At some stage later in the night, one of the women who was travelling with the soldiers went into labour. The locals were under the assumption that the parish would be forced to pay for the child's upbringing as a pauper, as was the law at the time. They wanted to cast her out and this caused an uproar which diverted the soldiers' attention from any other matters. The soldiers eventually left at dawn, after which Charles and his small retinue slipped away quietly and returned to the manor at Trent, near Sherborne, a place that had provided recent shelter for him and his small party.

The parish church in Broadwindsor, dedicated to St John the Baptist, is a beautiful Listed building that has many interesting features. It originated in the 11th century and there was some rebuilding in the 15th century, but it

The font comprises a square bowl constructed from Purbeck stone, with diagonal and chequer designs on its faces, moulded under the edge to take the rounded stem with four attached shafts, the whole placed on a moulded base of local stone.

The walls are heavily castellated, with some curious gargoyles.

was in the 19th century that major work was undertaken, changing the layout and appearance. Yet some parts of the older church remain, for example, the 12th/13th-century font.

In the churchyard is a real attraction. A mound, composed of years of tree detritus from an aged yew, thought to be more than 2000 years old. Fifteen trunks grow out of the mound, each of a size that indicates that they are approximately 150 years old. It would appear that during the rebuilding of the church in 1867 the yew was severely cut back to a stump. This was not enough to kill the aged tree but drastically changed its shape. It now has the look of a pollarded tree, truncated but with the special 'atmosphere' that ancient trees exude.

The ancient yew in the churchyard.

Yews figure in history and legend. The Magna Carta was signed under the spreading branches of a giant yew at Runnymede in 1215. Yggdrasil, the Norse Tree of Knowledge and Life, forming the Pillars of the Universe, was almost certainly a yew. Some of the ancient druidic sacred groves were thought to be composed of yew trees, and certain barrows that marked the graves of our ancestors in prehistoric times when opened were found to contain remnants of yew branches placed alongside the body.

The Fortingall yew in Glen Lyon, Perthshire, is a strong contender for Europe's oldest tree, estimated to be at least 5000 years old. Apparently, at Beltane on 1 May, fires were lit in a cleft in the trunk. This ancient yew, however, has a rival in the yew that grows in the churchyard of St Cynog at Defynnog, near Sennybridge, in the Brecon Beacons National Park in Wales. This tree has been dated to more than 5000 years old. It grows on the north side of the large ancient burial mound that constitutes a certain portion of the churchyard. This mound is likely to have been the last resting place of a late-Neolithic chieftain. There is another Welsh yew, dated between 4000 and 5000 years old, that grows in the churchyard of St Digain's church, Llangernyw, Conwy, North Wales. Although the core has rotted out, the huge girth makes this specimen an unforgettable presence. It was possibly planted in the prehistoric Bronze Age.

Ancient yews are often found in churchyards because the early Church was often established on pagan sites in an effort to eradicate earlier spiritual impulses. No other type of tree occurs so frequently within the grounds of churchyards. In some places, yews were traditionally planted to be close to churches, keeping up a subtly understood tradition. In other scenarios, yews preceded the church, sometimes growing naturally, sometimes marking an earlier, pagan, place of worship. An example of the latter is at Knowlton, near Wimborne in East Dorset, where there is a church erected within the banks of a Neolithic henge and near some 3000-year-old yews. It took a bold Christianity to build a church in such a site that was obviously dedicated to an ancient, raw and different originator.

The yew's capacity for great age led to it being seen as a natural emblem for everlasting life. The tree's quality of longevity and its ability to regenerate, where drooping branches that touch the ground can form new trunks, led to it being a symbol of regeneration and an emblem of the life-force. It is also symbolic of death, illustrated in the toxicity of its needles and the seeds found within its berries which can be fatal if ingested.

CATTISTOCK
Butterfly Reserve, Hill Settlements and a Holy Well

OS maps: Explorer 117 or Landranger 194

Grid refs: Cattistock roadside parking SY592996, Butterfly Reserve entrance and info sign ST610006

Directions: Cattistock is approx. 2 miles north of Maiden Newton off the A356 Crewkerne Road. Park in the centre of the village near the playground. Head east on foot along Duck Street, and where the road turns sharply right go straight ahead. Continue past a farmyard, with Castle Hill to your left and then Middle Hill. There is a footpath between them affording views of the earthworks but no formal access to either hill. Continuing along the valley past Middle Hill, you are now in Lankham Bottom and the Butterfly Reserve stretches up to the busy A37 on the ridge to the east. Back at the playground and pub, the church is obvious and the well is in the south-east corner of the churchyard by the path.

Cattistock is cited in *Domesday Book* as 'Ertacomestock' and was given its current name after the Norman invasion. To the east of the village is a special swathe of chalk downland known as Lankham Bottom. This area is leased by Butterfly Conservation and over 30 different types of beautiful and rare butterflies can be found here, such as the Adonis Blue, Marsh Fritillary and Grizzled Skipper.

Lankham Bottom is a nationally important reserve. The site is owned by Wessex Water and is a water catchment site for the local public supply. The grassland has been protected from agricultural 'improvement' and the natural, unsprayed grassland and wild flowers that thrive here encourage many invertebrates. Unimproved chalk downland is an extremely important environment for many forms of wildlife. Cattle lightly graze the grass and add to sensitive shrub control; this lack of overt management allows for an optimum environment for many insects. The fact that Nature Reserves and Wildlife Trusts, such as the one here and at nearby Kingcombe Meadows, part of the Dorset Wildlife Trust, seem to be gaining momentum is encouraging. Most people want to enjoy and would like their children to enjoy a countryside that has some life to it. Although unrealistic to expect modern farming to radically change, there is now a call for some sort of restoration of the countryside and more regard for the creatures that live within it. This is not to damn machinery

Lankham Bottom Butterfly Reserve.

but to strike a balance between food production and the requirements of a living landscape.

There is a small circular earthwork situated on Castle Hill above Cattistock which was likely to have been used by the Romans as one of their camps. This structure is known as 'The Castle' and it consists of a roughly oval enclosure of approximately 4 acres. On the highest part is an eroded mound, probably the remains of a tumulus, and other remains of ancient earthworks are situated on adjacent Middle Hill, immediately to the east. There are traces of Celtic field systems represented by low banks and also very faint remains of hut hollows of the same period.

The situation of Castle Hill is, as an 18th-century diarist might put it, 'exceedingly pleasant'. In times past, the old ridge road known as Long

The view to Middle Hill.

Ash Lane (now the A37) that runs to its east would have seen a variety of travellers – from Neolithic hunting parties, Roman legions, drovers, domestic animals and riders on horseback. The modern vehicles that now travel these downland heights, often on the old ridge routes, move so fast that little is seen or smelled. The fine downy air, with the sweet fragrance of flowers, grasses and warming earth, is lost to the inhabitants of cars. We forget how much, particularly in the summer, we miss of the countryside experience when we lose the scent of the land. Walking on the old paths, we can regain this. The scents, sights and sounds of the rural outdoors are doubly sweetened by the fact that they are not experienced as a common occurrence. When country people worked the land, the smells and sounds were part of life's expression. To only a small proportion of the populace is that now true, as most of us are insulated from the wider expanses of the countryside by the vicissitudes of our working lives.

The seasons play a big part in country pursuits and the one time of year when the festivities are particularly poignant is Beltane or May Eve. It is probable that most villages and towns had their maypole. A maypole was regularly erected outside the Fox and Hounds pub in Cattistock until 1835. However, in 1649, after the execution of Charles I and with Oliver Cromwell and the Puritan Roundheads now firmly in power, it was decreed that every maypole in the land was to be destroyed. After the Restoration, some maypoles were re-erected, including the one in Cattistock. Some of the old customs connected with the ceremony were probably lost in the time that had elapsed, but the festivities were still popular in many towns and villages, and the flower-bedecked pole, with its multicoloured ribbons, was the focus for much dancing, music and gaiety.

There was also the Cattistock Feast, a remnant perhaps of the benevolent custom of feeding the poor which was probably started by monastic houses in mediaeval times. Over the years the Feast expanded to provide amusements as well as physical succour. There was horse and donkey racing, wrestling, bell jingling and many other bucolic activities which made this event one of the most important of the country year, pulling in people from far and wide. Now the village has a Dorset Knob Throwing and Food Fest, with many different stalls and activities, including throwing the knobs, a sort of light, dry, hard ball of biscuit normally eaten with cheese. The person who throws the knob the furthest wins a prize, but the main prize, in many ways, is the enjoyment that many people have of getting together and having a happy and light-hearted time.

The church, as always, plays a part in community cohesion and there has been a church in the village since early times. Monks of Milton Abbey built the first church here in the 12th century, apparently on a Saxon site, and there are fragments of an early 11th-century cross set in a recess in the north wall, to the left of the altar. Other interesting early artefacts are a probable late

The font cover by Temple Lushington Moore is a grand folly that dominates the baptistry.

13th-century tapering stone coffin lid set in the east wall of the south aisle and, in the same area, a portion of 12th-century moulding and a chamfered stone bracket.

The church is dedicated to St Peter and St Paul. It was, to a large extent, rebuilt by the then incumbent in 1630, but over the next two centuries it fell into decay, until it was rescued by Sir George Gilbert Scott and his son, who practically rebuilt it in the 19th century. Sir George was an English architect who favoured the English Gothic Revival style of architecture. The church is now a good representation of Victorian Gothic, and the Perpendicular-styled tower has led to it being named the 'Cathedral of the Frome Valley'.

Left: the lovely William Morris window, partly designed by Edward Burne-Jones, in the south nave aisle.
Above: a carving on the door (significance of the Green Man is discussed in the chapter on Upwey).

A well is found in a corner of the churchyard, near the path that runs alongside the cricket pitch. This has all the characteristics of a holy well. Steps go down to clear water running under a stone arch which could have been designed by the Scott *père et fils*, as it looks to be 19th century. There is an atmosphere of peace here. This well was not just somewhere people came for water but a place that might have been sanctified years before the church was built.

Holy wells are often of great age, with some established in pre-Christian times when water was venerated for its health-giving properties and used for blessings. In early Celtic Christianity, missionary monks and nuns were often associated with springs and wells. They would site a small stone hut or

St Andrew's Well.

hermitage near the waters and baptise people into the Christian faith. The dedication of this well to St Andrew is possibly indicative of waters linked with baptism. He was the brother of Simon Peter and both were fishermen on the Sea of Galilee. Andrew met John the Baptist and possibly this was the reason his name is linked with the well, which could have been used for baptisms in early times. St Andrew became the first disciple and the first apostle and it was he who brought the boy with the loaves and fishes to Jesus, helping to enable the feeding of the five thousand.

The kennels for the Cattistock Hunt are tucked away on the eastern edge of the village, but the hounds there are often heard. The hunt was established by a parson living at Cattistock Lodge in the mid-18th century. It was originally known as 'The True Blue Hunt' because of their blue livery.

CERNE ABBAS
Abbey Vestiges and a Holy Well

OS maps: Explorer 117 or Landranger 194

Grid refs: Cerne Abbas roadside parking SY665012, Giant view parking SY663016

Directions: Cerne Abbas is 8 miles north of Dorchester, just off the A352 Sherborne road. Parking can usually be found in the village centre along Long Street. From the Royal Oak, take Abbey Street past the Pitchmarket, church and peaceful Squibb Garden. At the end on the right is Village Pond and in front South Gate House. Between them is a gate leading to the Guest House and Abbot's Porch, with a small fee payable. Another gate to the right leads into the burial ground. A plaque on your right gives the history of the well. Take the lower path to the end of the wall, then follow the small path down to the well. The yew is a little further into the churchyard, with some interesting graves nearby. If you don't wish to walk up to the Giant, there is a parking and observation area just off the A352 at the northern edge of the village.

The old Pitchmarket.

The fine building of South Gate House.

A Benedictine abbey was founded on a previous Saxon monastic site in Cerne Abbas in 987 by Ethelmaer, Earl of Devon and Cornwall. Here was written the beautiful illuminated prayers, hymns and biblical extracts of the *Book of Cerne*, now safely ensconced in the library of Cambridge University. Here too were produced volumes of Biblical translations and precepts by the reforming monk Aelfric, who attempted to render Christian truths into a language that could be understood by those who had little or no education.

Over the years, the abbey at Cerne grew in wealth and

status. Established families would endow abbeys and churches with much augmentation and richness in the hope that these bequests would open the Door of Heaven. Cerne Abbas was no exception, and the fine buildings, lands and precious books and artefacts gave the abbey high status. There are two tithe barns in the village, one north and another to the south-west (both now converted to private homes), showing how wealthy and important the abbey was.

Remnants of some of the fine mediaeval buildings survive. The impressive 16th-century Abbot's Porch, all that remains of the Abbot's Hall, reveals the craftsmanship that so blesses ecclesiastical buildings of this period. Tall oriel windows, ornamented stone shields and carvings of fantastical creatures serve to remind us of the skill and dedication that infused the master masons of those times.

The striking Abbot's Porch, built in 1509. (Photograph by permission of Captain and Mrs Fulford-Dobson.)

The Dissolution of the monasteries closed the majority of the ecclesiastical houses in Britain. Although some of the monks found succour elsewhere, many were cast out 'into the wilderness'. For those used to an ordered life of prayer and routine, this must have been an enormous test of faith. Some would take up the challenge and have the strength to transmit their living faith into all that they did. Others might be lost, struggling in an alien world in which they could find no purchase, their reality being too firmly embedded in the disciplines of church and cloister. Sometimes these poor souls would cleave, even after death, to the religious houses that once gave them their livelihood and their reason for being.

The Guest House was built around 1450 and would have housed travellers and pilgrims.

The Guest House, plainer but no less impressive. (Photograph by permission of Captain and Mrs Fulford-Dobson.)

The site of the church once connected with the abbey is now just a graveyard found close to the holy well. In the 7th century, a holy man, St Edwold, born of a Mercian royal family, lived in a small hermitage nearby until his death in 671. Apparently he had been drawn to the well by a vision.

There is another story about the well. St Augustine, accompanied by 40 monks, was sent to Britain by Pope Gregory in 596. At some stage during his mission to convert the natives to Christianity, he apparently found himself in Dorset. At Cerne Abbas, legend has it that he struck the ground with his staff and a body of water issued forth. This spring was named St Augustine's Well and a chapel named after the saint stood over the well. This lasted until the 17th century. The legend about the founding of the well is typical of the early approbation of a probable pagan holy site into a Christian one. The well is meant to work 'wondrous cures'. It has a triple reputation, as an oracular well, a healing well and a wishing well. Legend suggests that, in the past, new-born babies were dipped in the waters with the rising sun of dawn, and the waters were meant to protect them from disease and injury.

As you first approach the well, to the left of the pool is a square stone with an eight-petalled flower or wheel carved upon it – a remnant from the chapel or perhaps the abbey. The wheel has connotations with St Catherine, who has a chapel dedicated to her on a hill at nearby Abbotsbury, and apparently there was also a chapel dedicated to this saint on a hill south of Cerne Abbas

St Augustine's Well is also less well known as Silver Well, perhaps evocative of the moon's reflection in its still waters, or the name may come from Silvanus, a Roman Pan-like god.

that has now been lost. Others prefer to see it as a symbol of the pagan wheel of the year, marking the eight festival days of seasonal celebration. The stone by the well was known as the wishing stone. Girls would come to the well at sunrise on May Day and look into the well, hoping to see the face of the man they would marry. A grimmer version of this rite was linked with sunrise on Easter morning, where the face or faces seen would be of those who were to die within the year. There is or was another well in Cerne Abbas on the outskirts of the village, which was known as the Pill Well. This also was reputed to have curative properties, but its exact whereabouts have now become vague.

The wishing stone by the well.

Earthworks lie immediately north-east of the abbey site which consist of enclosures with banks and ditches. There is insufficient evidence as yet to explain their function, but hopefully future research will reveal the purpose of these interesting landscape features. There are also the eroded remains of small prehistoric camps in the area. The incised giant male figure that decorates the side of Trendle Hill ('Giant Hill') is too well known to qualify as 'secret', although his origins are still a matter of debate. My feeling is that the figure dates from

Earthworks on the hill above the graveyard.

the Iron Age and depicts the god of life-force and fecundity, Cernunnos. What is rather less known is the square banked earthwork above the giant, known as the Trendle. Although probably prehistoric in construction, it was used in historic times as a place where, on May Day, a garland-festooned maypole was erected, constructed from a local pine.

On the dawn of 1 May, a local Morris group meets here. They come complete with the Dorset Ooser, a strange barbaric mask that is worn, representing a presiding Lord of the Dance. This huge mask is a copy of the original which disappeared many years ago. In 1975 a similar replica was produced by John Byfleet, one of the Wessex Morris Men. This is now on display in Dorset County Museum in Dorchester.

Dancing in the rising sun on the Trendle.

The situation of Cerne Abbas embodies varying types of religious and ritual significance. The spring that feeds the holy well has probably been a feature of this landscape since the demise of the Ice Age, although it is difficult to gauge exactly when it was given religious recognition. The prehistoric earthwork which gives its name to Trendle Hill was possibly the first ritual construction in the area, although there are the other aforementioned 'lumps and bumps' in the locality which defy easy description. There is also the yew tree in the churchyard, not far from the well, which looks to be many hundreds of years old.

The abbey remains, Giant, well and yew vie for precedence, the Christianity of the one versus the old pagan lore of the others. The pagan nuance of spirit and place was the original sanctification of this area. Often Christianity moved in to areas that were already numinous, with the implied revelation that spirit always lies at the core of matter, whatever religion it serves.

Some interesting gravestones near the yew tree (below) and the remains of a 15th-century hamstone preaching cross (right) in the graveyard.

CHARMINSTER
Wolfeton House –
an Ancient Family Home

OS maps: Explorer 117 or OL15, or Landranger 194

Grid refs: Charminster roadside parking SY678927, Wolfeton House entrance SY678917

Directions: Charminster village is approx. 1 mile north of Dorchester, straddling the A352 Sherborne road. The entrance to Wolfeton House is half a mile north of Dorchester off the B3147, just before the A37 Dorchester bypass roundabout. Check opening times as Wolfeton is normally only open from June to the end of September, 2–5 pm, Monday, Wednesday and Thursday.

Charminster is situated on the outskirts of Dorchester, east of the River Frome. There are various points of interest within the village and its surrounding area. On the downs to the east is an area of Celtic fields. A tessellated pavement found nearby in 1891 indicated a Roman villa site. The bridge straddling the River Cerne by the church has mediaeval origins, although the arches that span the river have been rebuilt to prevent the frequent flooding and subsequent damage to the church. The church, dedicated to St Mary, has links with Wolfeton House in that in the early 16th century the tower was rebuilt by Thomas Trenchard, a member of an ancient family with strong links to the house. His monogram is carved on the west buttress. There are also monuments to the various members of the Trenchard family within the church.

Wolfeton House lies surrounded by meadows at the southern edge of the village. The building is a fortified manor house, and the ménage of different

Ancient Wolfeton House.

ages and various iconographies of style and construction that comprise the building serve to emphasise the unique feeling of the place. This site, near where the River Cerne joins the Frome, was probably first developed in Saxon or possibly Roman times. Nothing visibly remains from those early times, but the round towers on either side of the gatehouse are thought to be the oldest parts of the house, probably dating to the 14th century.

The gatehouse.

Various old Dorset families have been connected with Wolfeton, such as the Jurdains, Mohuns and Trenchards. Now the Thimbleby family, whose influence on the building has been subtle and benign, inhabit the house. They have seemingly effected little change on the accoutrements, beyond furnishing the rooms. The ornate decoration adds a certain grandeur to the house without diminishing its ancient charm.

The original courtyard section of the house dates to around 1480, when the estate was passed to John Trenchard. It is thought that the house was built on the site of a Roman structure, but there is no absolute proof of this. Most of the current building of Wolfeton was built in 1505 by Sir Thomas Trenchard and the

The Great Hall.

house is a good example of the architecture of the reign of Henry VII. It was updated in the time of James I by another family member, Sir George Trenchard, who extended the south range and embellished the building with the addition of some beautifully decorated fireplaces and ceilings and some fine panelling.

The Elizabethan and Jacobean carving, oak panelling and plastered ceilings are some of the finest in the country. The great stone stairway, built around 1580, is another stunning piece of craftsmanship. Although all the rooms open to the public are of huge interest, the Great Chamber is alone in still retaining its 16th-century floor. It also displays a fine carved fireplace, decorated with interesting figures including Native Americans. It is thought that Sir Walter Raleigh, who was one of the first Europeans to meet them,

Some of the beautiful carvings in the house.

must have given details of how they looked to the stone masons, who added their interpretations to augment the other, more traditional embellishments of the fireplace. Further changes and alterations over the centuries have remained largely in keeping with the original ethos of the house.

The Great Chamber.

Ancient houses have many stories to tell, but one of the most dramatic is the episode whereby an immense storm in 1506 caused the ship carrying Archduke Philip of Austria and his wife Joanna, daughter of the reigning monarchs of Spain, Ferdinand and Isabella, to seek shelter in Weymouth harbour. Sir Thomas Trenchard heard of the couple's misfortune and invited them to stay at Wolfeton. He was rewarded with gifts of a pair of Chinese porcelain bowls and some medallions.

Wolfeton was home to the Trenchards until the end of the 18th century, when the building was sold to cousins of the family, the Hennings. The maintenance of the house proved too much for the resources of the occupiers, and the fact that the chapel was starting to fall down and other parts of the building were beginning to follow suit necessitated some form of rescue. In 1862 the house was sold to W.H.P. Weston, another cousin, who had the funds to restore the parts of the house that were failing. The present owners, the Thimblebys, who are related to the Trenchards, took over the house in 1973.

The family has had to share their house with various ghostly visitants. Apparently the headless ghost of a past Lady Trenchard dressed in grey, who committed suicide at the end of the 17th century by cutting her own throat, haunts the Great Chamber. A ghostly coach and pair, driven by a past member of the Trenchard family, gallops and clatters its way up the main staircase. A Catholic priest haunts the gatehouse where he was sequestered for a while before being hung, drawn and quartered in Dorchester.

These were the Elizabethan times that saw Catholics as being sympathisers with Philip of Spain, with whom England was at war. Catholics were thus

The grand staircase.

considered traitors and had to practise their faith in secret. In various large houses the family priest was hidden, who then secretly ministered to the family through 'priest holes', as church-going was too dangerous a business for any to risk. Many priests were winkled out of their hiding places and executed, but a lot of them were able to remain hidden, emerging when political times were more equable towards the Church of Rome.

At the rear of the house is a building like no other in England – a Grade II-listed Riding House that dates back to 1605, where both horse and rider were trained in the art of equestrian skills. For some years it had been used as a barn, as when the estate was divided in the 19th century this building became part of the farm. However, in recent times work started to restore the building to its old status as a riding academy. In April 2014 the project was visited by the Duke of Gloucester and Mrs Anthony Pitt-Rivers who inspected phase one of the restoration project. The initial phase included consolidating the walls, reinstating the attic floor, opening up long-blocked windows and repairing some of the stonework. To find a building surviving from this time and seeing it brought back to life is one of the subtle rewards of a visit to Wolfeton.

The Riding House at Wolfeton.

CHEDINGTON
Lofty Vistas

OS maps: Explorer 117 or Landranger 193

Grid refs: Memorial parking ST491060

Directions: Chedington is approx. 5 miles south-east of Crewkerne, on the A356 Maiden Newton road. Turn right into Chedington Lane at Winyard's Gap Inn. The war memorial is in woods above the pub and has its own parking layby. The village is just 500 m further along the lane. There are several footpaths to access the River Axe beyond the village, but parking along the lane is limited. You might prefer to follow the 4.5-mile Beech Circular Walk detailed at the pub, taking in Chedington, the River Axe and the area covered in the chapter on Beaminster Down.

Chedington is situated near Winyard's Gap, a pass cut through the hills that divide this part of Dorset from Somerset. The wooded ridge on which the village is situated affords far-reaching views across Somerset. The village is blessed with one of the finest outlooks in the West of England and the view takes in the distant Mendip Hills, the Blackdown Hills, Ham Hill and the undulating fields and wooded areas that make up the rest of the landscape. The Brit Valley Way below follows the path of the meandering River Brit over a distance of 11 miles, from West Bay through to Chedington, culminating in a fine view of Dorset.

View towards Chedington from South Perrott.

There used to be many chalk pits at Chedington, some of which were used in prehistoric times. There was a resurgence in their use in the 19th century, especially around Langdon Farm. Chalk was an improver of certain soils and pulverised chalk, often with the addition of lime and manure, was put on grassland to increase the pH of acidic soils.

The National Trust owns a portion of land here, with a memorial dedicated to those who perished in both World Wars.

The main house in the village is Chedington Court, which was built in

Chedington Court.

mock-Tudor style in 1840 and is set in grounds of 31 acres, which include the source of the River Parrett.

The neighbouring River Axe rises south of here from springs around the two Axnoller Farms, and flows through Dorset, Somerset and Devon and into the

The River Axe starts as a stream flowing through woodland.

English Channel at Seaton in Devon. It has not the wild torrential energy of the ragged foaming rivers of Wales or the rock-strewn living dance of Dartmoor's clear browning waters. As it grows in size towards Seaton, this river has the ebb and flow of a lowland water, solid, structured and calm. The current glides through the countryside with sedate power, shaped by meadow and wood. Trout swirl in the eddies as the river widens and a few salmon come here to spawn, entering the river at Seaton and making their way through the deep waters to their secret spawning grounds up river.

The salmon is a fish that is surrounded by myth and legend. The name comes from the Latin *salire* – to leap. The largest salmon caught in Britain was in 1922 by Miss Georgina Ballantine, in the River Tay in Scotland. This mighty fish weighed 64 lb. The Celts associated the salmon with wisdom and there is an Irish myth about the place where the mysterious salmon of knowledge dwelled, swimming deep in a well called the Well of Segais. A magical hazel tree grew above the well and as the autumnal hazel nuts fell into the water, the salmon would eat them, increasing in knowledge as it did so. Whosoever had the skill to catch and eat this salmon would have knowledge of the future. In Welsh Arthurian tales, Llyn Llyw is a British lake that was home to great and magical salmon, the oldest and wisest of animals, which guided Arthur's warriors on a quest. Salmon appear in Pictish stone carvings, and although knowledge of this ancient culture is minimal, salmon evidently played an important part in the lives of these mysterious people.

CHESELBOURNE
Lyscombe Chapel

OS maps: Explorer 117 or Landranger 194

Grid refs: Grass parking area ST733004, Chapel ST736011

Directions: Lyscombe Chapel is approximately mid-way between Cheselbourne and Piddletrenthide and is best accessed from the latter. Heading north through the village on the B3143, take the right turn to Cheselbourne and proceed uphill for approx. 2 miles to Thorncombe Farm on the left. Turn into the third drive on your left, signed Lyscombe Farm, and park immediately on the grassed area to your right. This is a designated parking area and there is an information board. Proceed on foot down the farm drive for approx. half a mile to the chapel. Visit in the early morning or evening for a heady dose of atmosphere.

Lyscombe – a small, deserted place with a special atmosphere.

The name Lyscombe has been recorded since Saxon times and means 'reeds' and 'valley'. This place has always been an ecclesiastical hamlet rather than a village and is a secluded place, remote and slightly lonely in its position at the end of a farm track, but not bleak or lowering. Benedictine monks from Milton Abbey founded this chapel, choosing a situation that was sheltered and watered. These monks lived in the house adjoining the chapel (now derelict). It is thought that the monks built fishponds nearby where they would have kept carp for the table.

There is a story that the chapel is haunted, but details are sketchy. It is easy to affix ghostly visitants to remote places and buildings, it adds to their 'colour', but in the case of Lyscombe, the place does have rather an unearthly feel. The modern time tends to decry hauntings, but in the ages before the trappings of today's world, superstition and a belief in the supernatural were very much the norm, particularly with country-folk. Walking home at night, either from work or a visit to the local inn, would be the time when the senses would be more alert than usual (although that could be a moot point after a visit to the pub), and no doubt there would be places that would be either avoided or treated with caution. No one liked walking near the old gibbet sites at night or places where a battle had been fought or passing a lonely graveyard. Very few of us would have these sorts of experiences nowadays and we have become inured to the night-time experiences of the countryside, except perhaps when camping. A whole world has become lost to us, a world that could perhaps be unsettling but which also has texture and a certain sort of spiritual currency.

The chancel and nave are divided by a Transitional Norman arch with massive rounded columns.

Lyscombe chapel lies in the bowl of a particularly beautiful valley, Lyscombe Bottom. The chapel (dedication unknown) dates from the 12th century and is built of flint, stone and large blocks of rock chalk. The building was part of the endowment of Milton Abbey and was mentioned in 1311. It passed to Sir John Tregonwell in 1540 during the Dissolution of the monasteries at the time of the Reformation. In the 17th century it is thought that the chapel became a dwelling. It later became a farm-worker's cottage and a bake-house. In the early 20th century the nave had a large open grate, oven and

Ruinous cottage beside the chapel.

chimney in the centre. The chancel was used for storing logs and a flight of stone stairs led to bedrooms above.

The adjacent cottage would have accommodated the priest. In the 17th century it was enlarged by an addition to the west, so that the building doubled in size. It is now ruinous. There is a nearby barn which is mainly mediaeval.

Today the Dorset Historic Churches Trust does a fine job of looking

after the building. In 2005, the chapel was sensitively restored, using traditional materials of lime mortar, masonry, green oak carpentry and thatched roofing. The restoration won the RIBA Design award in 2006 and a Civic Trust Award in 2007. The former Bishop of Sherborne held Communion at the chapel to celebrate its restoration and revival.

Lyscombe has a feeling of remoteness which is in keeping with its status as a bastion of simple devotional faith. It is also placed in a beautiful setting. Whatever shape one's spirituality or even disbelief in spirituality takes, it is hard to ignore the succinct influence of 'place'. The siting of the chapel incorporates water, hillside, meadow and valley which together form a balance of subtle harmony.

An example of sensitive restoration work.

CHILCOMBE
A Tiny Churchyard and Iron Age Hillfort

OS maps: Explorer OL15 or Landranger 194

Grid refs: Roadside parking SY527913, Church SY528911

Directions: The most direct route to access Chilcombe is from the A35 between
Bridport and Winterbourne Abbas, but the road is very busy and the turn difficult
and unsigned, opposite the road to Askerswell. Therefore we advise approaching
from the south. From Bridport take the B3157 towards Abbotsbury. After Burton
Bradstock petrol station take the lane that bears left to Litton Cheney. After approx.
2.5 miles turn left at the crossroads to Chilcombe. Drive uphill past Rudge Farm, then
along the left edge of the wood which hides Chilcombe House and church. A little
further on you come to open downland and there is an area suitable for parking
near the bridleway sign.
　　To visit the church and see the house, leave your car and walk along the farm
track heading east. Back at your vehicle, Chilcombe Hill is to the north. There are
footpaths either side of the hill, but a circular walk is not advised because
of the busy A37. The bridleway to the east side is more sheltered and
peaceful.

Chilcombe House is situated within a copse of mature trees growing on the
northern edge of the Bride valley. The Tudor house that once stood here was
demolished, and the house that replaced it in 1728 is not without interest.

Close by is a small church, with parts dating from the 12th century. Within
the churchyard is a grey stone cross covering the grave of Frederick Samways
1803–1880, a tenant farmer. Frederick was a member of a well-established
Dorset family who married into another local family, the Gales. He must have
been a skilful farmer, because he enlarged the main barn in 1898 when there
was an agricultural depression.

Bones have been found to the west of the church, indicating that the
churchyard was once much larger than it is today. There is a small encasement
in the west of the church housing a single bell. Built originally for a congregation
of about forty, the church lost its clergy during the Black Death.

Entrance to the church is through the south door. Any dedication is
unknown. The building is a medley of different ages and styles. The walls are
composed of rubble, with the south wall of the nave being 12th century and the
chancel probably of the same period. The chancel arch, however, is later, being
14th century and the north and west sides of the nave are almost certainly
15th century, with some window glass dating from the 15th century. The 12th-
century Norman font is made of limestone, the stem and base being modern.

The rectangular churchyard at Chilcombe is one of the smallest in the country.

There is an interesting oak arm-chair, the wood blackened with age. This piece of furniture was made to commemorate the memory of Robert Bishop who once owned the manor, and RB 1642 is carved into the backrest. In the south-east corner of the chancel is a niche indicating a rare piscina.

The gilded coat of arms above the door is likely to be the arms of either the Strong or the Bysshop (Bishop) family, the latter being particularly associated with Chilcombe and holding the manor for many years. The stone lintel from the original Tudor house, inscribed 'John Bysshop, Eleanor Bysshop Anno Domini 1578', used to be in the chancel, from which it was stolen, but is now built into a stone garden arch a short distance to the west of the house.

The chair may have been in this position for more than three and a half centuries!

Note the engraved wooden panel fixed upon the north wall. Local legend attributes it as Elizabethan and coming from the Spanish Armada. However,

The present owner of the house is of the opinion that the panel is 15th-century Italian and was part of a chest used to bring church vestments from Italy to Britain.

recent opinion is that the worked inlay is stylistically English and possibly one of a tableau of three, the other two missing panels possibly representing the birth and ascension of Christ. This particular panel pictures the Crucifixion and was restored and remounted in 2000. It is believed that there are only three similar panels in this country.

Later in its history in 1832 the house passed to the 2nd Earl Nelson, a nephew of Admiral Nelson. Chilcombe belonged to the Trafalgar Estate until the very early 20th century. In the 1930s it was purchased by the Norton family, and is now owned by the landscape painter John Hubbard and his family. The old house was of two storeys with stone walls and a thatched roof and apparently incorporated parts of an earlier building; the north and south doorways were probably mediaeval. The present house is attractive and sits well within its setting. The garden is extremely well tended and complements the surroundings with colour and beauty.

Chilcombe Hill stands 200 m high above the complex and comprises approximately 20 acres. It has an Iron Age enclosure on top of it, with crop marks showing the presence of at least nine roundhouses. Such Iron Age hillforts, very occasionally built on an earlier Neolithic site, are scattered over southern England's chalk hills in reasonably large numbers. The fact that such ancient edifices can still be seen today is partly due to much of the upland being grazing land. Those parts of the land that have been put under the plough still tend to avoid many of the old hillforts, partly because the banks and ditches make ploughing difficult. The earthwork here has low inner and outer ramparts, with the remains of three entrances, and is an irregular pear shape, surrounded by a 2-m-deep ditch. Along the south-east side the defences now consist of two scarps with a small ledge between them. Within the enclosure is a probable barrow.

On top of the barrow at the north end of the enclosure is a prone sarsen stone and this could at one time have been a standing stone. Burnt flints and pottery have been found in the proximity of the traces of the roundhouses. The views of the surrounding country are extensive, with distant views of Golden Cap and other landmarks.

Chilcombe Hill.

In October 2007 a couple walking their dog on Chilcombe Hill encountered a black, panther-like animal, 'half as big again as our black Labrador' with rounded ears and a long, sweeping tail. It gazed at them and then went on its way. It was one of several sightings of big cats in the area, and there have been many such sightings in Dorset and indeed Britain as a whole.

There are many theories about the provenance of these creatures. Most ubiquitous is that they are escapees or released animals – though their predominantly black colouring, and ability to evade both capture and photographers, militates against this. More likely is that they are related to the 'Black Dogs' of West Country folklore – creatures that slip in and out of physical existence, confounding witnesses and attempts to categorise them. Either way they present an interesting existential problem to modern sensibilities, one which Merrily Harpur has explored extensively in her books *Mystery Big Cats* (Heart of Albion Press) and *Roaring Dorset: Encounters with Big Cats* (Roving Press).

None of these creatures has been known to harm humans, so be alert when you go up Chilcombe Hill, take a camera, and – you never know – you could be lucky! Chilcombe well rewards a visit. The narrow lane that winds up from the Bride valley leads to a treasure-house of beauty and interest in a forgotten world. The complex of church, house and farm buildings, coupled with the ancient hillfort, in a setting that is at once discreet and historically vigorous, combine to produce a combination that is both rarefied yet accessible.

CORSCOMBE
A Moated Court

OS maps: Explorer 117 or Landranger 194

Grid refs: Corscombe roadside parking SY526054

Directions: Corscombe is accessed from the A356, Maiden Newton to Crewkerne road. There are three turnings off this ridge, so take the one signposted for Corscombe and Halstock. As you enter the village, the church and Corscombe House are to your right. Continue downhill and Corscombe Court is on your left, 50 m past the Fox Inn. Parking is limited and on road. The Court is private, but there is a footpath, forming part of the drive, which passes close to the house and moat. You can also see the moat from further along the lane.

Corscombe is a small strung-out village lying in the hollows of the northern slope of an area of chalk downland. Like many of the villages in the district, all the elements that made small communities self-sufficient, such as the village school and shops, have now disappeared, and, apart from in a couple of the houses and outlying farms, very few born and bred Dorset people now live in the village. However, the beauty of the position of this small settlement, set

Corscombe Court is a house with deep historical connections, which help give cohesion to the local community.

55

within a diverse countryside of small hills, woodland and diverse dips and valleys, mitigates to an extent the absence of the original inhabitants.

Corscombe Court was formerly the grange of Sherborne Abbey and is a 13th- to early 14th-century building. The original grange forms the north wing of the current structure and contains a porch on the west side and an ancient lancet window. This wing was modelled internally in the 17th century. The south cross wing was built in the early 18th century and has a stone mullioned three-light window. The house is of two storeys with a stone and state roof.

The 15th-century tithe barn.

A beautiful tithe barn is situated in the private courtyard of Corscombe Court. The building has buttressed rubble walls and a south-facing porch and is thought to have been thatched originally. It is, along with the barn at Abbotsbury, one of the best preserved barns of this type in the area. Such a barn was used in the Middle Ages for storing tithes, which represented one-tenth of a farm's produce. These barns were therefore usually connected to the village church or nearby religious house, in this case Sherborne Abbey. Local farmers took their tithes to the barns and the revenue exacted would support the village priest, plus upkeep needed for the church and any religious house in the area. There are other fine examples of tithe barns at Abbotsbury, Glastonbury, Bradford-on-Avon and Pilton.

The moat which originally totally surrounded the buildings has been partially filled in on the south side. However, most of the moat can still be appreciated, particularly as it still holds enough water to allow for a small boat. It is thought to be the only water-filled working moat in the county of Dorset. The moat luxuriates in a verdant setting and the rich foliage that decorates the banks and the gentle tranquillity that emanates from the waters create an atmosphere that is somehow steeped in history, yet timeless.

There are other moats in the area. The dry remains of a square moat called

The moat at Corscombe Court.

Homestead Moat lie in a field called Court Ley about 1.5 miles south-east of Corscombe, near but not surrounding Benville Manor; maps also show a moat just to the south-east of Benville, but unfortunately neither has public access. Other Dorset moats are discussed in the chapter on South Perrott.

Buildings, such as Corscombe Court, which have ecclesiastical links act as a focal point, as does the church, for the community of which they are a part. Although Corscombe Court is a private residence, it plays a large role in the village. The annual summer fete is held in the grounds, with various stalls and activities, including boat trips on the moat. It is probably the oldest building, or set of buildings if the barn is included, in the area and the sense of historical worth and gravitas produced gives meaning to the sense of 'inviolateness'.

No one can doubt the reason why Corscombe Court was built. The premise was one of the distribution of religious solace and spreading of spiritual largesse that filtered through the auspices of Sherborne Abbey. Those who served in the Abbey, including the clergy who lived at Corscombe, were part of an important social framework. This gave many people a heightened sense of belonging to an exclusive spiritual enclave whilst also being part of a community that had actively been a constructive part of the area for generations.

EVERSHOT
An Ancient Oak, St John's Well and Stone Seat

OS maps: Explorer 117 or Landranger 194

Grid refs: Evershot roadside parking ST576046, Well ST572046, Red Post ST553040

Directions: Evershot is 13 miles north-west of Dorchester just off the A37 Yeovil road, and also clearly signed off the A356 Crewkerne road. Parking is generally available throughout the village, but near the stone seat and Melbury Park entrance at the eastern end makes a good starting point. Red Post is approx. 1 mile west of Evershot.

Evershot is the second highest village in Dorset, the highest being Ashmore on the edge of Cranborne Chase. The name 'Evershot' has various connotations, one being that it is derived from 'Eafor's Holt', meaning wild boar and wood. Probably the area was heavily wooded at one time and many boars would live in the arboreal fastnesses, providing good if dangerous hunting. Hunting was strictly regimented in mediaeval times, with boar hunting being the prerogative of the nobility. Apart from providing meat, the animal was hunted by nobles in order for martial skills to be honed. It was traditional for the hunter to dismount from his horse once the boar was cornered and dispatch it with a dagger. Otherwise it would be killed by a mounted horseman with a spear. The boar was a highly dangerous animal as it would fight ferociously when attacked and could easily kill a man, dog or horse with its tusks.

There is also the belief that wild boar were penned in this area, with a settlement building up in the proximity. The countryside would have suited early human habitation, for although reasonably elevated, the land is not too open and bleak, and is sheltered from the worst of the weather. Woodland would have been sourced for building materials and fuel, and the burgeoning river provided water.

For many years Evershot has been connected to the Melbury Estate. Melbury House is situated in Melbury Sampford on the edge of Evershot. The house has a Tudor core with a late 17th-century wing and later 18th- and 19th-century additions. The mansion has been the seat of the Strangways family since the estate was sold in 1500 by William Brouning to Henry Strangways. His son, Sir Giles Strangways, rebuilt the house sometime after 1546, using local hamstone. In 1692 it was extended, with some alterations, by Thomas Strangways and was

Melbury House is a private family home set in beautiful open parkland.

again further modernised in the 19th century.

Melbury Park surrounds the house and within its large expanse is a deer park with lakes, farms and large areas of woodland. The parkland is amongst the most beautiful in the county. The little church of Melbury Sampford near the house serves the family. It is not often open, but on occasions when it is, it is possible to visit some fine monuments, dating from the 14th to the 19th centuries.

Billy Wilkins, named after William Wilkins, a 17th-century bailiff employed by Sir John Strangways, owner of the Estate at that time, is the name given to an oak growing in Melbury Park. With a girth of 11.6 m, this tree grew here in mediaeval times, before the creation of the park. It is listed in the annals of historic trees, and although it cannot be viewed as it grows within a private part of the estate, it is good to know that such a special tree exists.

Trees that survive beyond the normal time scale and have been saved from the forester's axe seem to develop tangible personalities. They are given names, if only to denote their function, such as those huge oaks known individually as the 'Bible Oak' which serve as a focus for the community. Bible readings or open-air services used to be held under the spreading branches of these mighty trees, which seemed to emanate a subtle arboreal blessing. In East Coker, just over the border into Somerset, an ancient elm survived until recently. It was blown over by the storms of 2013 and now lies forlorn as a huge hulk in a field, a truncated leviathan ready for the sawmill.

In 1865 there was a great fire in Evershot in the area of Summers Lane which started in a carpenter's workshop. It destroyed eighteen buildings and left over a hundred people without a home, though there might have been more losses were it not for the close proximity of the river.

The village has various connections with Thomas Hardy. In 1893 Hardy was involved in designing an extension for Summer Lodge, which had originally been built as a dower house in 1798 by the 2nd Earl of Ilchester. The house is now a respected hotel. Evershot is portrayed by Hardy as 'Evershead', and the village pub, the Acorn, was the Sow and Acorn in *Tess of the d'Urbervilles*. The former name of this pub, once a coaching inn, was the King's Arms and it used to brew its own beer, using pristine water from the nearby spring.

This spring, St John's Spring or Well, is the source of the River Frome and can be visited by taking Back Lane which runs to the right of the church. After a few hundred metres there is a cleared area on the right with a structure displaying information about Evershot and the well. In a corner behind a low wall can be heard the sound of running water, issuing from a narrow gap below the wall. This productive well provides millions of gallons of water to the area. It is probable that the dedication is that of St John the Baptist and at one time it was used for baptisms.

Summer Lodge, formerly a dower house built in 1798 by the 2nd Earl of Ilchester. Hardy as an architect was commissioned to draw up the plans for the new second floor.

The source of the River Frome in Evershot.

There is an interesting signpost a couple of miles west from Evershot (marked as 'Red Post' on the OS map, at the bottom of Horsey Knap). It points to East Chelborough and is coloured red. Finger posts or signposts were widely used in Britain by the 1740s, with the oldest still in use dating from 1669 situated close to Chipping Campden in Gloucestershire. Only Dorset, Devon, Somerset and Cornwall have the occasional red post. Various theories have been put forward to explain their colour, including that these posts mark the site of a gibbet. Another explanation is that they mark routes used by prisoners on their way to port for transportation to Australia. Another possibility is that they mark the site of a battle. The red post near Evershot is said to mark the spot where, in the Civil War, Parliamentarians were ambushed by Royalists. The site is said to be haunted, although by what it is not clear, possibly the sounds of a battle.

Dumb Maids Plot, a field in Melbury Park near an area known to be the ancient musketry range of Stutcombe Bottom, is where legend says three dumb sisters used to meet and dance on the green. Dancing maids, particularly those who danced on the Sabbath and who were turned to stone for their audacity, were often a euphemism for standing stones and it is likely the three stones that form the strange seat under the tree at the entrance of

An ancient resting place.

the Estate road to Melbury Park originally came from that particular field. They could perhaps be the remnants of the forecourt of a long barrow. They now provide seating for the resident or visitor, and, although in all probability moved from their original position, are at least still offering some sort of service to the community.

The church is dedicated to St Osmund, and not to St John, as might be thought, and was originally 'a chapel of ease' for neighbouring Frome St Quintin. The first church on this site was Norman. Very little remains from that period, apart from the 12-century font basin which stands on a 19th-century pedestal, the chancel arch, part of the tower arch and the piscina.

There is an interesting brass plate on the north wall of the chancel which depicts a former rector, William Grey, who held the living from 1511 to 1524. These sorts of brasses are rare, with probably only two surviving in Dorset and only twelve in the whole of England. Another person of interest is George

Crabbe, rector of the parish from 1783 to 1784. He is regarded as one of the best rural poets of the time and depicted country people and rural life with compassion and realism.

Left: the Green Man is represented in carvings at the base of windows either side of the porch and one by a west window round the corner.
Right: brass engraving of rector William Grey, holding a chalice.

Evershot remains a village that is both welcoming yet faintly mysterious. It has been settled for hundreds of years and has the benefits of being in close proximity to an ancient established family and the wondrous parkland that surrounds a noble house. A fine river, the Frome, has its birthing in the village and the undulating countryside is satisfying on many levels. Yet under the surface there is the feeling that more goes on in this community than is immediately apparent.

EYPE
Down and Coast

OS maps: Explorer 116 or Landranger 193

Grid refs: Eype Down roadside parking SY439927, Lower Eype Church SY556878

Directions: Take the A35 Bridport bypass from West Bay roundabout. After approx.
1 mile turn left, signposted Eype. Ignore the rest area to your left, and after a
short distance turn right to Higher Eype. Continue uphill for approx. 2 miles, and
as you leave a wooded area and the road flattens there is limited parking space
on the right. A footpath opposite leads onto the down. The parking area can be
approached from the north, directly off the A35, half a mile east of Chideock, but
the turn-off is difficult on the brow of the hill and the road is busy. For the church, go
back to the bottom of the lane, turn right, then right again for Lower Eype.
The lane is often narrow, but there are car parks near the beach.

The word 'Eype' means 'steep hill' or 'steep place' and accurately describes the
terrain around here. Higher Eype is a hamlet tucked away in the hills above
coastal Lower Eype. Eype Down looms over Higher Eype and stands at 155 m,
one of three hills that dominate this part of the coast. The other two are
Thorncombe Beacon and the highest, Golden Cap – this cliff top attained its

View west across Lyme Bay, with Golden Cap and Langdon Hill in the distance.

singular name for two reasons: it was the site of one of the Armada beacons and there is a top layer of golden sand, its 'cap'.

There has been prehistoric activity in this area, with a bowl barrow on Eype Down and three more on Thorncombe Beacon near the coast. A recent archaeological dig on Thorncombe Beacon revealed Mesolithic flints. The prominent barrow between Eype Down and Thorncombe Beacon plays an important part in the scenery here, for it introduces a touch of the sacred working within the landscape. Eype Down would have suited settlement (although none has so far been discovered) as there are views from here of all the different elements of the surrounding countryside, including marine. There is a feeling of airy spaciousness, with the beauty of the varied hills and silvered gleam of the sea a satisfying meld.

Bowl barrow on Eype Down.

There is also a little-visited area of common land at the north end of Eype Down. This is an unfrequented piece of countryside away from the cliff paths.

Eype Down, with views north to Quarry Hill (left) and Colmer's Hill (right).

A tumulus can be seen and there are fine views, including the unmistakeable Colmer's Hill, topped with its small crown of pine trees. This common has rough shrubs, gorse and trees, indicating a landscape that has been largely left to its own devices. There is a smallholding where the land dips down to a cleared grassy area, but apart from this there is no indication of any great change that has occurred here, and the land is all the better for it.

Follow the paths down through a wooded area, heading south, bright with bluebells in spring, and Downhouse is reached. This is an ancient settlement with period buildings, a tenanted farm owned by the National Trust and part of the Golden Cap Estate. Since 1995 the farm has been organic and is managed under the Countryside Stewardship scheme, which works towards protecting plants and wildlife by adopting areas and unobtrusively caring for them. The farm has a cafe, a little-known haven of good food within pleasing surroundings, which is open between March and October. This is one of the area's secrets and is best found by walking down from Eype common, as Down House Lane through Higher Eype has a tendency to be pot-holed, with few passing places, making driving somewhat unnerving.

Old fair-ground carriage in the woods at the south-west corner of Eype Down.

There are an intriguing mix of old cottages in Lower Eype, scattered along the narrow lane that runs down to the sea, and even a converted railway carriage

Pretty cottages and gardens in Lower Eype.

that goes by the name of Railway Cottage (a Dream Cottages holiday home), opposite the pumping station. The church is now redundant for services but has been used for other purposes since it was closed for religious use and is now called Eype Church Centre for the Arts. During Dorset Art Weeks there is normally an art exhibition in the light and airy building. Corscombe-born singer and recording artist P.J. Harvey has used it as a recording studio, and various people, including the writer Virginia Ironside, have given talks inside the church.

The beach has a strange repose, being unhindered by beach huts or other buildings, and what is here are just the features caused by water and wind. The seaside scene is typical of the area, with unstable cliffs and shingle. There is nothing, apart from occasional washed-up debris, that speaks of human intrusion. Waves beat on the shingle, gulls swirl and cry overhead, and the wind and sun bleach the driftwood that lies scattered above the shore-line. This is the Jurassic Coast, revealer of aeons of time captured in strata of rock.

View east from Thorncombe Beacon.

FLEET
Wrecking, Smuggling and Storms

OS maps: Explorer OL15 or Landranger 194

Grid refs: Fleet roadside parking SY633805, Chapel SY634803

Directions: From Weymouth take the B3154 road towards Bridport and Abbotsbury. At the small roundabout on the outskirts of Chickerell, turn left to Fleet. After just 500 m, at the bottom of the hill, the old church is off to your left, after the row of cottages on Butter Street. There is no parking here, and signs encourage visitors to continue on and park at the second (new) church, on the right. The Fleet lagoon is easily accessible from the old church.

Chesil Beach is a pebble expanse that stretches from Portland to West Bay. The stones that comprise the beach are larger at Portland and slowly decrease in size as you head west. This is due to the wind and wave action, which batters the more exposed western shore but is gentler on the less-exposed east. A microclimate is produced by the lagoon called the Fleet, one of the results of which is the ability for plants to survive that are normally found in much warmer climes. This has resulted in the Subtropical Gardens at Abbotsbury.

The beach here can have a foreboding aspect and many a ship has fallen foul of the weather and unpredictable tides. The seabed is littered with wrecks that have foundered on this seemingly innocuous but deadly piece of coastline. Because of this, Chesil has a reputation as the bone beach of wrecks. The vagaries of wind and current were responsible for some of these disasters, but certain ships were lured to their doom by wreckers. Lights were placed so that the shoreline gave the impression of a safe harbour, but the vessels, thus tricked, would founder in the treacherous waters. The ships often ended up sinking close to the beach and within reach of a people who had little respect for life but much regard for what they could salvage from a stricken boat.

Smuggling was a way of life for many during the 18th and 19th centuries. Taxes on imported goods, such as brandy, tea and tobacco, were high in order to raise funds for expensive skirmishes with the French and Americans. Smuggled goods were free of this taxation and demand was brisk. The Dorset coast and Fleet lagoon were ideal for this profitable but risky trade and, with 18 miles of beach, smuggling was endemic in this part of Dorset.

Fleet lagoon, looking south-east.

A large proportion of this area of Chesil Beach is broken by the Fleet. Light is reflected from the waters obliquely; held in a reflective stance, it seems to glow with a strange transparency. This is a dreamy place, somehow different from both the sea and the surrounding countryside. This somnolent tidal lagoon is a verdant wildlife preserve which supports freshwater and brackish-water species. It attracts a huge number of water birds and includes the oldest Swannery in the world at Abbotsbury, at the far western end of the lagoon.

The Fleet is a unique body of water and there are very few similar in Britain. One such is Slapton Ley in Devon, another is Loe Bar, near Helston in Cornwall. The latter is a shingle bank that separates a large freshwater pool, the Loe, from the sea. It is much smaller than the Fleet, but, even so, is still the largest freshwater lake in Cornwall. Like many landscape anomalies, the Loe has accrued some folk tales. It is reputed to be the lake into which Sir Bedivere cast King Arthur's sword, Excalibur. Another such place at Trent is discussed later in this book. There is also the grim prediction that Loe Bar claims a victim every 7 years. In 2014, a local fisherman, John Coupland, said that the beach should have a skull and crossbones sign put up, after yet another body was found on the grim shore. It is a killer because it is steeply sloping, with large waves and a strong undercurrent, forming a deadly mix.

The Fleet does not have such a grim reputation, but there is the strange tale of the fox that walked on water. Running for its life and closely chased by the

Cattistock Hunt, this fox escaped the hounds by becoming a vulpine Christ, walking, or more likely running, upon the waters of the Fleet. This event was attested as fact by those of the hunt who had taken part on that eventful day. It apparently happened twice – once in the 19th century and again in the 20th century.

The Fleet has been largely protected from the sea's incursion by the high pebble wall of Chesil Beach. However, in November 1824 there was a tsunami and this natural sea wall was breached, leading to loss of life and devastation to the small village of East Fleet. Most of the village was swept away and the old church was largely destroyed, with only the chancel remaining. A heavily loaded merchant vessel, the *Ebenezer*, was picked up by the giant waves, swept towards the beach and with the force of the ocean deposited high on the gravel bank. Only two of the sailors drowned, the rest were saved, the waves that seemed likely to destroy them in the end becoming their saviour.

The church features in the novel Moonfleet, *where young John Trenchard is frightened by 'Blackbeard' Mohune's ghost in the family crypt under the church.*

A few cottages in Butter Street are all that remain of the old village of East Fleet. The neighbouring chancel was rebuilt and is a mortuary chapel to the old Dorset family, the Mohuns. On the wall is a brass memorial to Margarita Mohun, who died in 1603, leaving nine sons and eight daughters, and another to Maximilian Mohun. A replacement church was built for the little community, being completed in 1829, about half a mile down the lane and serving the hamlet of West Fleet as well as East Fleet. The new church is a good example of the Gothic Revival style.

The novel *Moonfleet*, written by John Meade Falkner and published in 1898, is based on the history of smuggling in this area and also the tragedy that occurred at East Fleet. Tales have been told that the phantoms of drowned sailors still walk the lanes of the village and surrounding countryside.

The Fleet is a place of strange beauty, with an atmosphere that is both brooding and intriguing. This in-between feature of a salted lagoon, so near the sea yet not of it, coupled with the immensity of the nearby briny waters creates a perceptible tension. There is a subtle coloration imbedded in this unique landscape which many find inspiring.

Separated from the sea by the stoney ramparts of the beach, Fleet lagoon is atmospheric in the way that in-between places often are.

HALSTOCK
St Juthware and an Ancient Way

OS maps: Explorer 117 or Landranger 194

Grid refs: Halstock village green ST539079, Church ST536084, Halstock Leigh ST511076

Directions: From Maiden Newton take the A356 north-west towards Crewkerne for 7 miles, then turn right to Corscombe. This lane gives perhaps the best, if rather distant, view of Birts Hill to your north, above Halstock Leigh. Continue on down the hill through Corscombe and a further 3 miles to Halstock. The Quiet Woman B&B is on your right just after the small village green.

For Higher Halstock Leigh, follow the signs from the village green. Just after the Village Hall there is a lane on your right to the church. However, continue on through Lower Halstock Leigh and after a couple of miles turn right for Higher Halstock Leigh and park appropriately further up the lane. It is pleasant walking through the hamlet, and you will see Birts Hill to the north-east. There are many footpaths in the area but none that goes up the hill itself.

The name 'Halstock' means 'holy outlying farmstead'. This is taken from the Old English 'holig' and 'stoc'. The settlement used to belong to Sherborne Abbey and was enabled because of a grant given by King Aethelwold. The early Christian community based here gave the area a sanctification, which subtly still exists in certain remote parts of this region.

Halstock is associated with St Juthware and there used to be a popular pub in the village named with a degree of humour, the Quiet Woman. The quiet woman was St Juthware herself, who in the 7th century was decapitated, at the decree of her stepmother who was jealous of the girl's apparent holiness. On the dawning of All Saints Day, at one o'clock in the morning, St Juthware's ghost is said to walk the lane leading to Abbot's Hill. That the hill is called

St Juthware is depicted in the stained glass window in the door of Quiet Woman House.

'Abbot's Hill' could be because of the link Halstock has with Sherborne Abbey. No ecclesiastical buildings have survived in the immediate area, but nearby East Coker reputably had a monastery and it might be that there was some link with the Halstock area. The fact that St Juthware was said to live in the vicinity also lends credence that there was a religious house of some kind situated on the hill and that house gave the hill its name.

The village has an interesting history. A Roman pavement was found in excavations directed by the Earl of Ilchester in about 1818. This pavement was on the north-west side of Common Lane, about half a mile from the church. It was described as having a geometric pattern of blue, red, black and white tesserae. The main design was a square set diagonally within a broad border, containing a circle in meander pattern. The corners cut off by the circle contained roundels framing helmeted heads, with cross staffs in the background. The large circle enclosed a star-shaped panel bordering a medallion, decorated with a head similar to the others but larger. Sadly most of it was damaged by treasure-hunters and what was left was covered and now remains underground.

A Romano-British villa was discovered nearby and excavated firstly in 1967 and later in 1985. It was located south-west of the old golf course just north of Common Lane and was in use around the 2nd century. It consisted of a rectangular complex of buildings and associated structures located around two courtyards. A field survey revealed the villa complex visible as slight scarping in the north-east of the field. It overlay a Late Iron Age settlement consisting of hut circles and a ditch complex. The Durotriges tribe who inhabited the dwellings lived in the Halstock area between 50 BC and AD 50.

There used to be two inns in Halstock. The New Inn was of 17th-century origin; although largely rebuilt, it retained two original stone-mullioned windows. It is now a farm, called New Inn Farm, and is found at the junction of Common Lane and Leigh Lane. The second inn was the Quiet Woman, which ceased to be a pub in the mid-1990s and is now a bed and breakfast. Also there was at one time a privately run lunatic asylum in the village which lasted until the mid-1800s. Halstock Village Shop and Post Office is now a community owned and run venture, serving Halstock and Corscombe.

Halstock's church is dedicated to St Juthware and St Mary. There is an interesting memorial in the churchyard to the right of the gate, commemorating John Pitt. He was known as 'Three Century Man' as he was born in Halstock in 1799, lived throughout the 1800s and died in 1901, aged 102.

John Pitt's grave in Halstock churchyard.

Halstock Leigh lies approximately 2 miles west of Halstock and is a quiet hamlet together with Lower and Higher Halstock Leigh, the latter ending in a no through road. Birts Hill overlooks these settlements, a large hill with a forested plantation covering much of it. There is a remote feeling to this area, which is near the Somerset/Dorset border. There are many footpaths here and several farms and the feeling that there has been minimal change, apart from some modernisation of the farms. Part of Birts Hill is called Dancing Hill and

Birts Hill, Halstock Leigh. View from above Corscombe.

this evocative name brings to mind May Day festivities and other rites celebrating the seasons' rounds. The secret of Dancing Hill and how it might have acquired its name are now lost, but we can imagine what frolics might have gone on there.

The Harrow Way, from 'hoar' meaning 'ancient', runs from the Kentish coast near Dover and enters Wessex at the Surrey/Hampshire border. It travels across the chalk uplands of Wiltshire, crosses into Dorset and finishes at the mouth of the River Axe at Seaton. The Harrow Way is called Common Lane as it passes through Halstock and Corscombe. This Neolithic route is one of the oldest roads in Britain, comparable to the Ridgeway. Curiously named Curry Hole Lane is another old track half a mile south of Halstock off the Corscombe road, which runs to the church at West Chelborough.

Curry Hole Lane has a tendency to be muddy at the West Chelborough end even in the driest of weathers, so waterproof boots are advised.

Sometimes these old paths were first formed by Palaeolithic wild animals and the hunters following them. They were later used as trade routes, as the west of England provided tin, lead, copper and iron, metals that were traded with the south and east of England and abroad. Ancient tracks have seen the movements of humans and animals over centuries and it can only be guessed what sort of people used them and what sort of animal. Domestic certainly, but also, in early mediaeval times, wolves and wild cats such as lynx. This combination of different types of travellers over vast periods of time creates an atmosphere that can be appreciated by anyone using the powers of imagination and sensitivity.

Britain has many old lanes and trackways, they are part of our history. They often followed natural contours and linked settlements and farmsteads, and were used for driving animals between grazing sites and to market in later times. Some trackways, also known as green lanes, would lead to religious sites such as long barrows, henge monuments and stone circles. Some were processional routes, such as the Avenue at Stonehenge, leading down to the River Avon. Later, various tracks became roads and they lost their footpath status, while others continue to be used by walkers and horse riders. The Ridgeway, Icknield Way, Harrow Way and Pilgrims' Way are amongst our most ancient well-known trackways. Some travelled on high downland, and consequently are known as ridgeways, often providing the core for later routes used by the Romans, and later still Anglo-Saxons, followed by Normans. Hilaire Belloc said in his book *The Old Road* (published in 1904) that of all primal things that move us, 'the least obvious but most important is The Road'. He was describing the Pilgrims' Way, which travels 120 miles between Winchester and Canterbury along a prehistoric trackway.

A pilgrimage is inexorably linked with the route that takes the pilgrim to the eventual place of high worth and sanctity. Mediaeval pilgrims, travelling for the good of their soul and hope of ensuring a place in heaven, would travel well-trodden routes. Over time, these accrued a miasma of holiness as they became deeper pathways, hollowed by the marches of dedication.

There are also lychways (paths of the dead) which are the routes used to take coffins to their place of burial. There would often be large slabs along the way, known as coffin stones, where weary bearers could place the coffin so that they might rest awhile.

In Roman times many ancient trackways were utilised and became foundations for the roads used for troop movements and commerce. These routes allowed the Romans ingress into the heartlands of Britain. In this way the old roads were the collateral that, over different centuries, lost the indigenous peoples part of their identity, as they were gradually fused with the different invaders into a homogenised whole. Although the Romans built many new routes, it was the old roads that cemented their conquest.

As Curry Hole Lane ambles through an old-fashioned landscape of sheep-grazed pastures, which in parts has a parkland feel, the track edges woodland and passes through areas of trees that provide pattern and shade in the summer months. Travelling along this path provides a sense of the past and the little-disturbed back-country.

Along old Curry Hole Lane at the Halstock (northern) end.

KINGCOMBE
Back to Nature

OS maps: Explorer 117 or Landranger 194

Grid refs: Kingcombe Centre parking SY553990

Directions: On the A356 Crewkerne road, approx. 4 miles west of Maiden Newton
and immediately before the large radio masts on Rampisham Down, turn left for
Hooke. At the bottom of the hill turn left at the crossroads. After 1 mile there is
parking at the Kingcombe Centre or a little further up the lane at the
DWT reserve site on the left.

Flower-rich grassland at Kingcombe.

The land that is now Kingcombe Meadows Nature Reserve used to belong to a farmer, Mr Wallbridge, who farmed his land as they did in the old days – free of almost any chemicals and without much man-made imposition. When he died and the farm came up for sale, there was a fear that the land would be bought as prime farming country and irrevocably transformed. Because of the wonderful biodiversity of this countryside there was a public appeal, supported by HRH the Prince of Wales, and most of the land was bought and saved. Now maintained by the Dorset Wildlife Trust, the land here is part of an old Dorset that is increasingly hard to find.

The 457-acre (185-ha) reserve is a mixture of small fields grazed by sheep and cattle. These fields include unimproved grassland, thick hedges, ancient green lanes, woodland, streams and the River Hooke. In spring and summer the whole area is abundant with wildflowers, sedges and grasses. Summer warblers, dippers and grey wagtails are amongst the smaller birds that frequent here, while larger birds, such as ravens and buzzards, wheel overhead, searching for a fallen fallow or roe deer to scavenge before the wild boar arrive. Wild boar have

River Hooke.

established themselves here and in nearby Powerstock. They have returned to the land where their ancestors roamed, ancestors that were eventually wiped out around the beginning of the 18th century. The progeny of escapees from farms, these animals tend to hide from humans and lie up in thick undergrowth during the day, foraging mainly at night.

At one time all our countryside was similar to this – no chemical fertilisers, fields kept small, areas of woodland contributing fuel and foraging for pigs, a wide diversity of vegetation, insect, animal and bird life, and a rural populace who valued their roots, held strong within the landscape. Life must have held different joys in those times and there is still a hint of that era here at Kingcombe.

Mr Wallbridge may not have realised that his way of farming was now becoming rare and that the agrichemical business, coupled with field and hedgerow clearances, were a suffocating edict to put upon the countryside. Using natural fertilisers (manure and compost), there were hay fields, grazing land and meadows where wildflowers, such as lady's mantle, devil's bit scabious and knapweed, grew freely. These provided nectar and pollen for the honey bees who had their hives amongst the apple trees in the orchard. He and his family would have been almost self-sufficient with their food, fuel and water.

All the seasons experienced at Kingcombe have their special beauties and joys, but possibly autumn is the most rewarding. The land is fruitful with blackberries and fungi in the fields and woodland. The Dorset Wildlife Trust runs foraging expeditions at this time of year and people are encouraged to join these groups and learn how to pick mushrooms and wild herbs safely. Wild food has a special satisfaction, something that food bought from shops will never have. It tastes fresh and good, and when we develop the ability to recognise what is edible within the countryside, a certain sort of freedom is also accessed.

The Kingcombe Centre is a cluster of buildings spread around a garden area and small pond. Here talks and courses are run, both day and residential. There is also a lovely conservatory café open to the public at certain times, serving homemade and home-grown food, and even foraged fruits. The Centre's location in this unspoilt countryside inspires many and one of the briefs here is to inform people about the countryside as it once was. The Centre has its own vegetable garden, honey bees and livestock and very much practices what it preaches.

The fact that Kingcombe was saved from intensive farming and has now become such a beacon of inspiration gives credit to the vision and perseverance of those who managed to raise the money for its purchase. Not only does it throw light on how farming used to be, it also gives a template as to how

In the orchard at the Kingcombe Centre.

farming could be again. It is not intensive, it values the natural habitat and wildlife found therein, and employment is given to local people who care for the land here. There are those who work in the Centre, helping to organise the talks and activities, the accommodation and café. In all ways this is a success story but shouldn't be taken for granted. There are times when Kingcombe needs support, which should be freely given, for if we were to lose this rare and idyllic place, it would have reverberations reaching far deeper than what appears to be obvious.

The accessibility to an old-fashioned landscape that this area affords is of benefit to all who visit. To be amongst the rough meadows, hedgerows and areas of woodland and stream is to go back to the past, where farming worked in an intimate arrangement with the wildness of nature. To be able to still have access to this innate synchronicity is more than just a relic of past times, it is a way-shower for an understanding of what constitutes true fecundity.

LAMBERT'S CASTLE
An Old Fair Ground and 'Spirit Hole'

OS maps: Explorer 116 or Landranger 193

Grid refs: National Trust car park SY366987

Directions: From the A35 at Raymonds Hill (just north of Lyme Regis) take the B3165 towards Crewkerne. After approx. 4 miles, the entrance to Lambert's Castle NT car park is on the right, just before you drop down through thick woodland. The turning is easy to miss.

Lambert's Castle is an Iron Age hillfort that was probably constructed by the Durotriges tribe 2,500 years ago. The ditch and bank that constitute the 'castle' can be clearly seen at the western entrance. The fort is situated on the summit of the hill, which rises to 256 m. There are steep slopes on three sides and ramparts can still be seen across the southern part of the hill. The fort encompasses 12 acres and the contour of the hill is followed by triple banks and ditches, which are sometimes hard to discern as they are very worn in places. There is a possible barrow near the middle and also some post-Norman rabbit warrens.

There is much beauty in the terrain. The southern part of the hill is being allowed to revert to heather and gorse, something that is appreciated by glow worms, seen here in the summer months and adding to the special qualities of this fine piece of high land. The inspiring views are thought by many to be among the best in the county. Portland, Chesil Beach and the Fleet can be seen

Springs rise on the hill and these would have been a factor in the siting of a fort here.

On the ramparts of ancient Lambert's Castle.

as well as the Devon coast and, in the far distance, the uplands of Wiltshire and Somerset. There are wonderful views of nearby Marshwood Vale, with valleys, meadowland, hills and woods. In the distance the vision is culminated by the shimmering luminosity of the sea.

Between 1709 and 1947 an annual fair was held here on the Wednesday before the feast of St John the Baptist on 24 June. In the 18th century, as part of the fair, the hill was also used as a racecourse. A local family, the Herberts, restarted the fair, but it proved not to be financially viable. Traces of the racecourse can still be seen south-west of the hillfort.

An anonymous 17th-century historian stated that this hillfort was haunted but did not say by what. A report by a 19th-century local Reverend gentleman notes that locals had recourse to a 'Spirit Hole' somewhere on the hill, where they used to commune with spirits. What form of supernatural visitant they communicated with is not given, nor is the location of this spirit hole revealed, except that it was somewhere on or near the top of the hill. It is difficult to fathom exactly what sort of 'hole' this might be – whether it was big enough to allow people to enter it or whether one just peered down into its murky depths. It would appear that it gradually fell out of use, probably because of a disapproving clergy. Whether it still exists, possibly in the centre of an impenetrable bramble thicket, or was eventually filled in is not known. Maybe one day the 'Hole' will be found and the spirits will commune once again.

The old name for Lambert's Castle was Lammas Castle. The name Lammas comes from the Old English 'hlaf' meaning loaf and 'maesse' meaning feast.

Earthwork ramparts and woodland of Lambert's Castle.

Lammas festival is celebrated in high summer on 1 August as a harvest festival, as August is traditionally when the wheat and barley is reaped. As the harvest is gathered in there is food for the community and seed for next year's crop. The harvest was seen as an aspect of the largesse of the Earth Mother and the living spirit of the grain was called John Barleycorn. As the corn is cut, John Barleycorn is cut down, surrendering his life so that the people can be fed. Like a Pagan Eucharist, he is both eaten as bread and reborn as the seed that returns to earth. There is a well-known folk song dedicated to him and it is often in music and song, some of these ancient, that the flavour of old country life can be appreciated. The tale of John Barleycorn is an image of immortality. The first sheaf would often be ceremonially cut at dawn, winnowed, ground and baked into the Harvest loaf which was then shared by the community. The last sheaf was also ceremonially cut and made into a 'corn dolly' which was central to the Harvest Supper. This last sheaf would be placed above the fire hearth until harvest the following year, when it would be winnowed back into the ground, enabling the fertilising influence of John Barleycorn to pass on from season to season. It is possible that the fair that used to be held here in June is a faint memory of earlier Lammas celebrations. Another name for Lammas is Lughnasadh (pronounced loo-na-sa), named after Lugh, the sun god.

Lambert's Castle is an exhilarating hill to visit with much to offer. The views in themselves make this a special place, but there is also the addition of the hillfort with its archaeological and cultural interest and the supernatural input of the Spirit Hole, plus cavalcades of fairies and diverse other alleged ghostly visitants. Depending on one's persuasions, this is either a place to certainly avoid at a full moon or one to definitely visit!

LEWESDON HILL
A High Fairy Place

OS maps: Explorer 116 or Landranger 193

Grid refs: Roadside parking ST439005

Directions: From Bridport take the B3162 towards Broadwindsor. After approx. 5 miles, and just after a crossroads with Stoke Abbott signposted right, you will see a few cottages and private lane to Brimley Coombe Farms on the left. There is a pull-in area, so park here and walk down the farm lane. Go through the gate on the right where a footpath leads up Lewesdon Hill.

> Up to thy summit, Lewesdon, to the brow
> Of yon proud rising, where the lonely thorn
> Bends from the rude South-east, with top cut sheer
> By his keen breath, along the narrow track
> By which the scanty-pastured sheep ascend
> Up to thy furze-clad summit, let me climb;
> My morning exercise; and thence look around
> Upon the variegated scene, of hills,
> And woods, and fruitful vales, and villages
> Half-hid in tufted orchards, and the sea
> Boundless, and studded thick with many a sail.

This excerpt from the poem 'Lewesdon Hill' written in 1788 by William Crowe could well be describing not just the immediate view but the whole of West Dorset. This was an important poem, being a precursor to the Romantic Movement.

In William Crowe's time the hill was covered more with gorse and pines rather than the beech trees of today.

Lewesdon Hill: a place of spirits and spirituality.

William was born in Midgham, Berkshire, and christened in 1745. His father was a carpenter and a man who apparently encouraged his gifted son. Under patronage, William was educated at Winchester College and then at New College, Oxford. He was ordained in 1773 and in 1782 presented with the living of Stoke Abbott. Here he stayed for just a few years, moving to Alton Barnes in Wiltshire in 1788, as the village was more convenient for Oxford where he still held many interests.

The hillfort is defended on its south-western and south-eastern sides by a precipitous scarp.

There is evidence of an Iron Age settlement on the hill, with its flat summit and enclosure of about 2 acres. At the west end are traces of a ditch about 7 m below the summit, with an outer bank, and there are various suggestions of filled-in ditches. A few metres east of the west entrance are possible traces of an inner rampart and the earthwork would appear to be the eroded remains of a hillfort. Unfortunately there has been much disruption to the area by gravel digging and timber extraction so that parts of the fort have been badly damaged. It also seems that parts of it may have been quarried away, as in the past there was a quarry here, excavating chert for building stone. A headwater of the River Char rises on the hill and water from this spring was once bottled and sold as 'Lewesdon Spring'.

Lewesdon is reputed to be a haunt of fairies. Some places seem subtly perfumed with the presence of the fae, who are often linked to a particular habitat and thought to be connected to the vitality of the land, in a similar way to country deities and nature spirits. According to Reverend Kirk, a Scottish folklorist born in 1644 and author of *The Secret Commonwealth of Elves, Fauns and Fairies*:

> *These Siths or Fairies they call Sleagh Maith or the Good People ... are Said to be of middle Nature between Man and Angel, as were Daimons thought*

to be of old; of intelligent fluidous Spirits, and light changeable bodies (lyke those called Astral) somewhat of the nature of a condensed cloud, and best seen in twilight. These bodoes be so pliable through the sublety of Spirits that agitate them, that they can make them or disappear at pleasure.'

There is also a 'firm identification between the fairies and the land', says R.J. Stewart, another Scottish author, born in 1949. Stewart wrote *The Living World of Faery* (amongst other works). The fairy tradition is a very specific one of contact between human and Otherworldly entities and has its own techniques and symbolic language. Fairies were often linked with particular prehistoric sites and landscape features and Lewesdon seems to have had its own particular band of strange unearthly beings.

There are also ghosts associated with Lewesdon. In the 1970s a woman who lived nearby walked up Lewesdon, accompanied by her two children. This was a walk that they often did, but this time the journey was different. Near the top of the hill, the woman was overcome by a nameless dread. Nothing could be seen but she knew she had to get off the hill immediately. She gathered her children and ran down the hill, fear accompanying every step. Again in the 1970s, another woman and her two children saw a headless horseman come out of a fog bank. It must have been a terrifying sight. Most world cultures have their ghost and fairy beliefs, even though modern culture is dismissive. It is unwise to banish completely the idea and actuality of other dimensions of being, because a one-dimensional world is then created, based entirely on

physical fact. The door is then shut, and shut completely, on a whole strand of life that has the potential of adding an extra dimension to our knowledge of what makes up our existence.

There have been reports of a large panther-like black cat and also a wolf seen in the area. West Dorset seems to abound with sightings of big cats and no one can quite say what they are. Mysteriously compelling, difficult to pin down exactly, the fact that one has been seen in the Lewesdon area adds to the mystery of this enigmatic hill.

Unusually for a West Dorset hill, Lewesdon is thickly wooded and its tree-strewn heights have a reputation as being a fairy place.

LITTLEBREDY
Secret Walled Garden

OS maps: Explorer OL15 or Landranger 194

Grid refs: Littebredy roadside parking SY587891, Gardens SY584890

Directions: Take the A35 west from Winterbourne Abbas and after 1 mile take the lane south to Littlebredy. Park at the round wooden shelter and walk down the no-through road to the Gardens. Opening times are 2–5 pm, Wednesdays, Sundays and Bank Holidays from Easter Sunday to the end of September. Sometimes rain will close the Gardens, so it is worth phoning if the weather is inclement.

The Bride valley is one of the most beautiful areas of countryside in West Dorset. Edged by undulating hills, this wide valley hosts the River Bride, which rises at Littlebredy, and is lit in the south by the closeness of the sea. A hilly ridge separates Chesil Beach from the valley, but this does not prevent the casting of the light that the sea gives to the immediate environment. This light is subtle but adds to the overall atmosphere that permeates this valley.

Littlebredy has a fine late 16th-century manor house which was enlarged and altered in the 1830s and 1850s. The house, known as Bridehead, is sited by a beautiful lake, created in the 19th century by damming the springs that are the source of the River Bride.

The secret garden of the title is the old kitchen garden that used to provide flowers, vegetables and fruit for the manor but which became redundant in the early 20th century. The garden was established during the Georgian period but was at its most productive during the Victorian era, when it was tended by 14 full-time staff. By the mid-20th century, labour costs, plus increased mechanisation which needed large fields rather than small areas of land, made the production of food no longer cost effective in the walled garden.

This garden used to be the productive heart of the Bridehead family estate and provided not only for the Williams family, who are the long-term owners of the Littlebredy estate, but also, to an extent, for the villagers. It is a 'lost' Victorian kitchen garden and is altogether about 5 acres, with the walled garden being a 1-acre plot which is being carefully restored to regain its past glories. The infant River Bride flows through the garden and adds the clarity of its living waters to enhance an already beautiful environment. The Bride valley has a warm microclimate which aids plant growth. The garden is also positioned on a south-facing slope, with plant health further aided by the shelter of the high walls.

Littlebredy Walled Gardens today.

The English garden is both an actuality and an idea. The idea of an English garden is that of a verdant inspirational mix of plants and environment which presents an idealised concept of nature. Whether as a large idyllic parkland landscape with a lake, grottoes, groves of trees and recreations of classical temples, such as Stourhead in Wiltshire, or gardens on a more intimate level, this idea had at its core the premise that gardens were food for the soul.

The actuality of the garden for most people is on a much smaller scale but still fundamentally a satisfying mix of flowers and shrubs which delight with scent, shape and colour.

The gardens at Littlebredy offer food for the soul.

The establishment of a garden is one of the most creative ventures that can be undertaken. It is the realisation of which plants work well with others, the rightness in terms of shape and colour and the added joys of scented plants, whose gifts so delight one of the more neglected of our senses.

The earliest English gardens were planted by the Romans and are typified by low box hedges split by gravelled walks, with niches for busts and statues. It was not until the monastic gardens in the Middle Ages that gardens regained some importance in British life. The Tudor period formalised knot gardens and the Stuart gardens were also tightly structured and more influenced by the formality of French gardens than English ideas. The 18th century saw a more natural look but with carefully calculated vistas and classical ornamentation, such as at Stowe. The Victorian era saw massed beds of flowers and taste varied between the formal and the informal garden, such as that seen at Sissinghurst Castle, Kent, and to an extent here in Dorset.

The gardens at Littlebredy are being restored as part of a community venture and there are full-time and part-time helpers who enthusiastically work with clearing, planting and propagating various plants, shrubs and vegetables for the good of the community. The old greenhouses, potting sheds and other tumbledown stone buildings are gradually being restored to their former usefulness and the whole area is a testament to vision and enthusiasm, with the results clear for all to see.

The Gardens were originally leased from the Bridehead estate by Chris and Judy Yates. They cleared and replanted the garden, and in 2008, when they retired, the Walled Garden Workshop was formed as a not-for-profit community venture and the Gardens leased by Liz Eaton and Chris Burr. Gardening and horticultural workshops aim to introduce volunteers to the basic principles of working with plants, giving practical experience which can help those looking to find a career in horticulture.

The attractive gardens and walks, restored for visitors to enjoy.

NETHER CERNE
A Bucolic Setting

OS maps: Explorer 117 or Landranger 194

Grid refs: Nether Cerne roadside parking SY670983

Directions: Nether Cerne is just off the A352 Cerne Abbas to Sherborne road, approx. 6 miles north of Dorchester. After Charminster, Forston and Godmanstone, the turn for Nether Cerne is on your right. There is limited on-road parking and signs to the church. The footpath heading north towards Cerne Abbas skirts the nearby lakes.

The river at Nether Cerne.

The manor house and Gothic church of All Saints.

This tiny secluded hamlet is sited on the banks of the River Cerne. The settlement is dominated by the 17th-century manor which unusually had a thatched roof. Rethatched periodically over the centuries, the roof lasted until early in the 20th century, when it was finally replaced by tiles. The manor and the adjacent church are built of bands of flint and stone. The hamlet used to be part of the endowment of Cerne Abbas Abbey which was served by Benedictine monks until the Dissolution of the monasteries.

The late 13th-century church is a redundant church in the care of the Churches Conservation Trust. The last service in this Church of All Saints was in 1968 and it was declared redundant in 1971. The nave, chancel and east choir are retained from the 13th century, with the tower, its pinnacles and the porch added in the 15th century. The Norman font bears a similarity to a bell flower or melon and dates from the 12th century. It is thought that the font remains from an earlier church which had been built on the same site. The current church was restored in 1876 and has seating for a hundred people.

Unusually, rather than gargoyles looming from the tower, there are eight angels.

The secluded setting of riverside meadows and rolling hills makes this a quintessential English scene. In a field approximately half a mile east of the church are the remains of an earthwork consisting of two banks which seem to be part of a rectangular enclosure. The north-east bank extends about 15 m and is roughly 4.5 m wide and just less than 1 m high. The slopes to the north and west are covered by a Celtic field system. There are old field barns and field patterns.

The Gallia family came to Nether Cerne in 1970 and created the lakes and planted 50 acres of woodland. There is also a herbal medical practice at Nether Cerne, run by Eleanor Gallia. This practice uses herbs grown on the family land, some wild-crafted and some grown elsewhere in certified conditions.

This hamlet peacefully dreams in secluded semi-isolation. The Galias have helped create a landscape of fecund beauty, and the river and lakes in particular bring a light and reflection that animates the surrounding countryside.

NORTH CHIDEOCK and SYMONDSBURY
Hollow-Ways and Healing Springs

OS maps: Explorer 116 or Landranger 193

Grid refs: Hell Lane roadside parking SY424938, Carvings SY433938

Directions: From the A35 in Chideock, approx. 4 miles west of Bridport, take the lane
to North Chideock. Ignore the left turn to Morecombelake and shortly after turn right
at the T-junction. As you drop downhill take the right fork and park appropriately
near the end cottages. Continue on foot up Hell Lane track to the east. If you are
unable to walk up Hell Lane, the Broadoak road out of Symondsbury is a
fantastic example of a hollow lane which can be driven by car.

In and about North Chideock can be found some of the old paths known as
hollow-ways. It is thought the term is Saxon and means 'harrowed path'. Some
of the tracks were pilgrim routes conveying the earnest seeker towards shrines

*Hell Lane – a chasm-like dark path that has hosted the movement of human and animal life
through the ages.*

and holy places where salvation could be found for the soul. Many of these paths are prehistoric and part of our living history. Sunk below the level of the fields, these ways have been worn down by centuries of footfall, the lumbering of wheeled vehicles and the eddies and transient streams caused by rainfall.

Hollow-ways can only be found in areas where there is sandstone, chalk, greensand and other types of soft stone. Some are more than 6 m deep, becoming chasm-like and more like a ravine. Sometimes the old hedges that were naturally seeded or planted alongside the path would, untended and overgrown, form a canopy overhead, filtering what light there was into a green and shadowy luminance. These eldritch ways are sunken wildernesses, some overgrown and unpassable, others like skeins in the landscape, redolent of earthen history etched by the footsteps of those long dead.

Hell Lane hollow-way is a continuation of the tarmacked Hell Lane that runs through North Chideock village. The derivation of Hell Lane could be referring to the dread nether regions, the abode of the dead or the Underworld, or it could be a derivation of Helios, an ancient Greek solar deity representing the sun. Names of places often become degraded over the centuries, so we can never be sure that a literal meaning of an ancient name is correct, but conjecture adds an intriguing aspect to exploration and can enliven one's appreciation of a place.

The unmade section of Hell Lane can get very waterlogged, and in all but the driest of weathers waterproof boots are recommended. Travelling up Hell Lane east towards Symondsbury, the path becomes drier the higher you go. Near the crossing of paths towards the crest of Quarry Hill there is an area where inscriptions have been carved in the sandstone sides of the track. Over time these have gained a weathered appearance but are still decipherable. The name 'Pan' has been carved and the great god who answers to that name would be at home here, trilling his pipes at dawn and dusk, his song echoed by the birds and winds.

Inscribed in the sandstone.

At the crest of paths known as Quarry Cross, turn right for a great view of Colmer's Hill from a field gate. Named after the Reverend John Colmer who owned the land in the early 19th century, the reputedly fairy-haunted hill is probably the feature that gave Symondsbury its name, as 'Symondsbury' derives from Old English meaning 'the hill or barrow belonging to Sigemund'. The Caledonian pines on top of the hill were planted during the First World War by Sir Philip Colfox in honour of his father, Colonel Thomas Colfox. The Colfox family has been associated with Symondsbury and Bridport since 1280.

View of Colmer's Hill from Hell Lane at Quarry Cross.

The hollow-way to the left of the gate continues downhill to Symondsbury. Here the high gnarled banks are criss-crossed with fissures, softened by branches of trees. There is a multitude of growing things, shrubs and trees and myriad plants, some liking gloom, others positioning themselves where sunlight can dapple them with light. A journey through these deep lanes is somehow an encapsulation of an arboreal jungle. Symondsbury has various other lanes of interest. The last section into Symondsbury is known as Shute's Lane and reveals various different types of geology. It is recognised as a regionally important geological site, with limestone, marlstone rock bed and occasionally ammonites.

The stream that flows through Symondsbury comes from a spring that is said to have healing powers. People used to come from miles around to bathe their eyes and many healings were meant to have taken place. The stream is a tributary of the River Simene which goes on to join the River Brit in nearby Bridport. One of the ancient lanes that passes through the village is an old pilgrim way taking pilgrims to the shrine of St Wite at Whitchurch Canonicorum, approximately 3 miles to the west. This was a place of great veneration, both for the healings that allegedly took place at the shrine in the church and for the veneration that holy St Wite had accrued over the years. The well of St Wite, a couple of miles from the church at Whitchurch Canonicorum, is also reputed to be a healing well, particularly for eyes.

These atmospheric ancient hollow-ways encourage spooky imaginings and there is a tale that a ghostly white cow was once seen in a field in the Whitchurch Canonicorum direction, not far from North Chideock. The white cow is an old British breed, and the rare and beautiful Chillingham Wild Cattle found in Chillingham Park, Alnwich, Northumberland, are the sole survivors of herds that once roamed Britain. White cattle were also associated with the fairies and were seen as Otherworldly beings.

The old routes across the countryside open up intimate vistas which are timeless in their meanderings. The primal seclusion that the ancient hollow-ways offer takes us back to the early stages of human ingress within the landscape. The old sunken trackways have now become part of nature and are a fascinating route to the heart of the countryside.

When returning to North Chideock, nearing the bottom of Hell Lane you may like to digress off to the right on a track where there is a tranquil pond and clear views of the hills surrounding the village.

Pond near Hell Lane.

PILSDON
Secret Hinterland of Pilsdon Pen

OS maps: Explorer 116 or Landranger 193

Grid refs: Layby parking ST414009, Pilsdon Church SY995415

Directions: Pilsdon Pen rises above the B3164 Birdsmoorgate road, approx. 2 miles west of Broadwindsor. The hill is clearly signposted and there is a layby for parking. For Pilsdon church take the narrow lane opposite the hill. Turn right after a short distance, then left in Pilsdon village. Parking is very limited, along the road near the manor.

The village of Pilsdon probably gained its name from the hill that rises approximately 1 mile to its north. This small village is composed of a church, manor, couple of farms and a few cottages. The manor house when under the ownership of Sir Hugh Wyndham, a member of a prominent local family who had lived in Pilsdon for many generations, was raided by the Parliamentarians during the 17th century during a fruitless search for Charles II in his cat-and-mouse flight from Cromwell's forces. The Monarch's Way passes through the village. Sir Hugh and his family, who were thought to be sympathetic to the king, were subjected to the dismal and unnerving experience of seeing and hearing their house being dissected from top to bottom. No king was found and the manor survived. Now it is home to the Pilsdon Community,

Pilsdon Manor (a private community, not open to the public).

a Christian organisation providing a refuge for people in crisis.

Pilsdon Pen is 277 m high and the second highest hill in Dorset, nearby Lewesdon Hill being taller by a whisker at 279 m. Neolithic flint tools have been found here, and Bronze Age burial mounds, predating the Iron Age hillfort,

The church is open at all times and services are held three times a day. Anglican by foundation but ecumenical in expression, people of any faith, or none, come together here.

are situated on the highest point of the hill. The fort comprises 9 acres and is enclosed by triple banks and ditches. In the centre is a tumulus surrounded by a rectangular enclosure, with four more tumuli at the southern end of the earthwork, and the remains of 14 roundhouses also near the centre. There are varying opinions as to the purpose of the square structures in the centre of the fort: they could be mediaeval pillow mounds which were created for breeding rabbits, or the remains of earlier man-made structures which have yet to be formally identified.

The approach to Pilsdon Pen is via a stile and path that runs steeply up from the road. The hill affords far-reaching views of the sea and Marshwood Vale, but the paths and ditches winding around the hillsides give a different appreciation of what this hillfort has to offer – this is the secret hinterland. Most of us, when subjected to a hill, make straight for the top and the views, and the flanks get overlooked, resulting in much of the hill's uniqueness remaining undiscovered.

Pilsdon Pen was bequeathed to the National Trust by the Pinney family in 1982.

Pilsdon Pen has had a long and varied history – a history that is intertwined with human endeavours over thousands of years, from the Neolithic onwards. In those ancient times people crouched on the side of this hill, knapping flints into useable artefacts, and it is possible to find flint scrapers here, a reminder of this. Later, in the Iron Age, vast quantities of earth were moved to form the defences of this fort, a fort that eventually failed against the Romans.

Cattle and sheep have made trackways around the hill, following the contours, and these add to exploration, for they travel through areas of natural peacefulness. Animal paths often follow magnetic energies that are found within the land. Small trees and shrubs grow alongside some of these paths; in fact the hill is far more wooded than would immediately appear. These tree-filled areas are essentially primeval, where vegetation and wildlife are allowed their own voice, largely free from human interference.

The Wessex Ridgeway, Jubilee Trail and Monarch's Way all converge on Pilsdon Pen.

There are places in the countryside where nature rules, where tangles of woodland bar entry to anything other than birds and wildlife. We like to think we can go and explore anywhere, but there are some parts where nature likes to be left to itself and we are wise if we accept that and do not intrude. Areas of Pilsdon have this quality, but there are also parts of the hinterland where the hill reveals itself subtly and rewardingly as a place of multidimensional natural beauty. It is up to every explorer to tread their own path and find the route that allows them to hear the hill's voice – there to appraise the possibility of understanding some of the subtle nuances of this many-layered place.

PORTESHAM
The Hell Stone and Bronkham Hill

OS maps: Explorer OL15 or Landranger 194

Grid refs: Hell Stone parking SY601868, Hell Stone SY604867, Bronkham Hill (start) SY616877

Directions: Drive up the steep hill out of Portesham towards the Hardy Monument, and as the road starts to level there is a small layby/verge to park. Follow the footpath east across the first field and over the stone stile. Proceed another 100 m, then go over the stone wall on your right at another stile. The Hell Stone is up ahead. If the layby parking happens to be full, park at the Hardy Monument and walk down through Benecke Wood to reach the second stone stile. For Bronkham Hill, drive on up to the Hardy Monument, with the option of its NT car park. Bronkham Hill is a short distance on past here, on the right, and there is free roadside parking.

Portesham is a small village which is a gateway to an area of landscape that is one of the most archaeologically important in Dorset. The village is an intriguing place with a history of supernatural occurrences, including the ghosts of a headless horse-rider and a headless man sitting on a gate. The small settlement is a focal point for the exploration of a diverse range of important prehistoric artefacts and places.

The landscape to the north of Abbotsbury contains many megalithic features, one of which is the Hell Stone. It is situated on Portesham Hill on the summit of a south-facing limestone escarpment with which it is aligned, the entrance facing the sea and midday sun. The 'Hell Stone' comprises not just one stone, as the name suggests, but nine large stones, including upright stones and the capstone which alone weighs around 16 tons. This Neolithic monument was probably erected around 4,000 BC and is all that remains of a chambered tomb, the mound of which would have been roughly 24 m long by 12 m at its widest point. In its original state this communal grave would have dominated the local landscape. Although only vestiges of the gravitas of the original tomb remain, what is left is sufficiently intriguing to warrant interest. As a feature and statement of past times this ancient edifice retains its mystery, helped by its setting in a landscape of downland and rough pasture. The enigma that the stones convey seems ageless.

During the 6,000 years since the grave was built, time took its toll and the structure became ruinous. The giant capstone had fallen, along with many of the supporting stones. By 1860 all the stones had mostly collapsed, and in

The Hell Stone is the most complete dolmen in Dorset, even though it is now only an approximation of what it would have been.

1866, the Reverend Martin Farquhar Tupper, together with a small team of quarrymen from the Isle of Portland, managed to resurrect an approximation of the original.

Reverend Tupper was fired by enthusiasm but had very little knowledge of the structure of long barrows. He was born in London in 1810 and died in 1889, was a Fellow of the Royal Society and had diverse interests. He published a book entitled *Proverbial Philosophy* which consisted of many pages of poetic moralising. Although a slow-burner initially, the tome eventually proved popular, being printed in 40 editions over 30 years and selling in many thousands in Britain and nearly a million in the United States. Although this work was widely dismissed as maudlin pseudophilosophy by critics and intellectuals of the day, Tupper was undaunted and published other works. He supported many reforming movements, including the Student Volunteer Movement, and had world-wide interests, African literature being one. Maybe his various enthusiasms were thought to give him a sympathy for the workings of the prehistoric mind and the structure of the graves those minds created.

Long barrows were mostly built during the period 4000–3000 BC, with most of them out of use by 2500 BC. They were seen as 'Houses for the Dead' and were communal graves for up to 60 people. Complete skeletons were rarely found, with skulls and long bones being the predominant remains. The bodies were divested of flesh before their remains were interred. This was probably achieved by excarnation, where the bodies would have been exposed in high places to the natural forces of dispersion and decay.

Burials in long barrows, and in the later Bronze Age the round and various other types of barrow, would have been of high-status individuals. It leaves the question as to what happened to the other 90% of the population when they died? Were they broken up and fed to scavenging birds, as in the Tibetan 'sky burial'? Were there vast cremation pyres? No traces in Britain have ever been found of the remains of the general ancient populace.

Local legend says that the Hell Stone was thrown to its current position from Portland, nearly 10 miles away, by the Devil playing quoits. This is typical of the stories that surround certain ancient structures and is probably a remnant of the Christian dismissal of the previous pagan spiritual traditions. Its name could have a variety of roots. 'Heelstone', which is a description of a capstone, could be one, derived from the Saxon 'Helian' – 'to cover or conceal'. It has also been called 'Stone of the Dead' and this idiomatic description could link to the Goddess Hel. In Norse mythology Hel featured in the 13th-century prose poem 'The Edda', a poem derived from earlier traditions. Hel presided over the realm of Hel or Death and this rightly ascribes the function of this ancient site as a last resting place for the dead. In Wales it was Arawn, God of the Underworld and war – the Underworld (also known as Annwn, Land of the Dead) was seen by Christians as Hell. In later traditions, the role of King of the Underworld was given to Gwynn ap Nudd.

Long barrows were not just repositories for bones but were almost certainly used for ceremonies which involved some sort of recognition of the Ancestors' role that continued to be played in life. Long barrows such as this one which could be entered were invariably situated in the east, the place of the rising sun. Thus they could be considered as portals where the shamans, early practitioners of healing and magic, could perhaps act as mediums, giving access to the Underworld.

There is a nearby long barrow, the Grey Mare and Her Colts, approximately 1 mile westwards, and there used to be another long barrow, much closer to the Hell Stone, which has now completely disappeared, the stones probably removed for building, with any mound flattened by tractors and the passage of time. There is a suggestion that there is a Processional Way, an ancient ridgeway path that connects the sites of the Hell Stone and, heading west, the Hampton Stone Circle, the ruined long barrow of the Grey Mare and Her Colts and Kingston Russell Stone Circle. This is largely now just a public footpath, but some years ago, large stones edging the path were found, suggesting that this route could have been a sanctified route, a Way of the Dead.

The Victorians used to visit sites such as the Hell Stone and would strike artful poses that would be sketched, or in late Victorian times photographed by early practitioners of the art. The Gothic Revival of the mid to late 19th century sought out places that typified the romantic qualities of gloom, towards which the Victorian mind gravitated. Places redolent of the sepulchre and features such as standing stones and other prehistoric sites, caves, the lowering mountain or the scary tangled wood provided stimulation for the darker recesses of the Victorian mind.

An unusual stile on Portesham Down.

About 1 mile north-east of the Hell Stone is Bronkham Hill. The hill is host to part of the 17-mile South Dorset Ridgeway and the much longer 625-mile South West Coast Path (inland route) National Trail. There were almost 250 barrows along the length of the Ridgeway, though some of them have been ploughed out. Alongside the track on Bronkham Hill, approximately 30 bowl and bell barrows are strung out on the skyline as visual memorials to our ancestors. These would have been white chalk mounds originally and must have been an impressive sight, gleaming in the sun and shining in the moonlight, way-showers for the dead and the living.

Bronkham Hill. In prehistoric times, bodies of the important dead, perhaps chieftains or shamans, would have been carried ceremonially to their burial site along this special route.

Death road, corpse way, ghost path and spirit way are all terms that could well describe this trackway that proceeds along the elevated crest of the hill. On the edges of parts of this fine track can be seen large flat slabs of stone. These are thought to be Saxon and they help delineate the trackway. The late Master Dowser Guy Underwood considered slab stones as markers for routes that were in some ways special or 'holy'.

This whole area is covered in barrows, which vary from small to very large – up to 30 m across. One of the largest of these is a bell barrow which has been bisected by the track. This particular barrow is surrounded by a bank and ditch, as is normal for this type of edifice. Bell barrows were first identified by the 17th- and 18th-century antiquarians John Aubrey and William Stukeley. They are similar to bowl barrows but differentiated by having a 'berm', a low narrow platform separating the mound from the surrounding ditch.

There are various holes in the area, known as 'sink holes'. These are a naturally occurring phenomenon, produced where the chalk has collapsed. The fact that many of these sink holes are found near to certain barrows and are similar to an inverted barrow, replicating in size and shape the nearby barrow but in reverse, adds strength to the idea that these particular landscape features were seen as portals, allowing access to the Underworld.

The Hardy Monument, erected in 1844 to commemorate Admiral Lord Nelson's friend and flag-captain Thomas Masterman Hardy, who was born in Portesham.

At least 40 Neolithic long barrows have been found in Dorset, dating from circa 4000 to 2500 BC, including some in the general area of Bronkham Hill. Yet there is no evidence of any Neolithic activity on any part of this ancient way, an area that was probably forested at this time. Perhaps time has erased any evidence.

The Hardy Monument on Black Down is at the western end of this part of the ridgeway, and the eastern part ends at the Roman road at Ridgeway Hill, now the A354 Dorchester–Weymouth road. From the monument, on a very clear day, it is possible to see Hameldown Tor on Dartmoor. An Otherworldly Black Dog is said to haunt the Black Down area.

PORTLAND
St George's Church
and a Quaint Museum

OS maps: Explorer OL15 or Landranger 194

Grid refs: St George's Church parking SY686721, Museum parking SY695713

Directions: Take the A354 from Weymouth on to Portland. Drive up through
Fortuneswell, then steeply uphill to the roundabout in front of the Heights Hotel. Bear
right for Easton, and St George's Church is approx. 0.5 miles on your right, with
parking just before it. For the Museum, head east from St George's into Easton. After
the gardens and playground in the centre of Easton, turn right at the T-junction and
follow the road for approx. 0.5 miles into Weston until you see the Museum
on your left. There is a dedicated car park a little further on on the right.

The unique headland known as the Isle of Portland is composed of the white
limestone that is named after this curious promontory of sea-girt land. Fine
views can be enjoyed from Portland – both to the east, where expanses of
Dorset cliffs backed by downland can be seen, and west, where the huge curve
of Chesil Beach and the strange stretch of water, the Fleet, leads on to West Bay,
Charmouth and the high eminence of Golden Cap.

Prior to extensive quarrying, starting in the 18th century, Portland was a
wild, rocky, somewhat barren strip of land, with numerous prehistoric features.
There were stone circles, standing stones and other early artefacts (see *The Spirit
of Portland: Revelations of a Sacred Isle* by Gary Biltcliffe). As this historic past
was gradually eroded away by the quarrying, Portlanders looked to churches to
provide their religious solace.

At one time St George's Church in Reforne was a premier church in Dorset
and certainly one of the most impressive 18th-century churches in the county.
Built between 1754 and 1766, it replaced the crumbling 15th-century St
Andrew's Church, situated on unstable land above Church Ope Cove, remains
of which can still be seen. Church Ope Cove was thought to be the scene of the
first Viking landing in England.

St George's Church was built on the edge of the hamlet of Reforne, near
Easton village. This was an elevated central position ideal for a new church
and there was also enough topsoil here to make possible the digging of the
required 6-ft-deep graves, a difficult feat on most of Portland which is mainly
composed of rock. The church was designed by a local man, Thomas Gilbert,

Built of the same stone, St Paul's Cathedral influenced the design of St George's Church on Portland.

whose grandfather owned the quarry that supplied most of the stone for St Paul's Cathedral.

Although magnificent in many ways, the church had always been thought of

The beautiful box pews were originally bought by local families on a freehold basis. By 1900, due to the unusual Portland laws of inheritance, hundreds of the original families' descendants had a claim on these pews. Several of the pews did not face the altar, which was not liked by the Bishop.

as cold and uncomfortable and, as the years progressed, the congregation slowly dwindled. The fact that soon after the church was built the pews were sold off to prominent local families for their sole use did not help matters, as some of these families were tardy church attendees and the pews were often empty.

In 1913, a new parish church was approved, to replace St George's. This new church, dedicated as All Saints, was situated in Easton and sounded the demise of the older church.

St George's gently mouldered, its condition not helped when it suffered a hit by a stray bomb in the Second World War. By 1968 funds were raised by the Friends of St George's and restoration commenced. When new legislation was introduced, St George's was one of the first four churches in the country to be placed in the care of the Redundant Churches Fund, which in 1994 became the Churches Conservation Trust. It is Grade I listed, with the large churchyard containing over a thousand graves being given a Grade II listing.

In 2012, £800,000 was spent on repairs to this special church. Services take place here on St George's Day and a carol service is held on Christmas Day. Real Portlanders still like to be buried in St George's churchyard.

The graves tell stories of murder, piracy and shipwreck, all part of the ferment of Portland's past.

Portland Museum is situated in the hamlet of Wakeham which lies above Church Ope Cove. The museum was founded in 1930 by Dr Marie Stopes, the pioneer of birth control. It is charmingly housed in two 17th-century cottages which had fallen into a state of dereliction before they were restored by Dr Stopes. These cottages add their own historic character to the museum, which displays an eccentric mixture of fascinating items of local history and archaeological finds. Four different areas are explored within the museum. They are Portland People, Maritime Portland, Portland Stone and Jurassic Portland. Examples of the latter two can be found in the garden of the museum with a collection of local fossils, including fossilised trees, and the stone remains from St. Andrew's Church.

Within the portals of the museum there are more important collections of fossils on show. There is a large collection of cycads, a type of plant that flourished during the Jurassic period. Here too can be seen examples of enormous ammonites and the fossilised remains of reptiles. There is also a real rarity, known as the Portland turtle. This is the oldest example of a turtle so far found in Britain. This specimen dates from 145 million years ago and was found in 2010 in a Portland quarry.

Some cottage rooms have been filled with period items which give an intimate portrait of how people lived in Victorian times and earlier. This is a museum which has been set up with imagination. There are display cases and brightly lit rooms, but there is also an intimate human quality which can give us an emotional appreciation of distant times, making them accessible and still part of our lives.

Opposite page: Portland Museum, with displays on the history of Portland Stone, shipwrecks and famous people connected with Portland.

PUNCKNOWLE
A Look-Out Station

OS maps: Explorer OL15 or Landranger 194

Grid refs: Church SY535887, Knoll parking SY537877

Directions: Take the B3157 coast road east from Bridport for approx. 6 miles. In Swyre, turn left for Puncknowle and after just half a mile park near the church. To reach the Knoll, drive on past the church and bear right along Clay Lane. As you ascend, the Knoll is the tree-topped hill to your right, but continue until the road flattens out and there is verge parking on the left. Take the footpath opposite which winds around and up the south side of the Knoll, to the old refuge. For the field 'Walls' take the opposite footpath/farm track downhill from the road.

Puncknowle is a small village attractively positioned on the southern slopes of the Bride valley and situated about a mile inland from the sea. The name is pronounced 'punnel' and the latter part of the name comes from 'knoll', a distinctive small rounded hill. The knoll in question is to the south of the village and from it can be enjoyed fine views of the coast and surrounding countryside.

For three centuries the Napier family, originating from Merchiston in Edinburgh, lived at Puncknowle and also held the manor of West Bexington. Robert Napier, born in 1640, was a Tory member of parliament and was knighted on 27 January 1681. He died at Puncknowle on 31 October 1700 and

The Jacobean manor house is adjacent to the church.

There are various monuments to the Napiers in the church.

Helmet of a knight of the Napier family.

is buried in the churchyard. A large monument to him can be found within the church. No later member of the family entered Parliament and eventually his son, Sir Charles Napier, sold the estate.

The manor house built by the Napiers was described by Frederick Treves (eminent surgeon and author of *Highways and Byways in Dorset*) as 'one of the daintiest and most beautiful manor houses in the county'. After the Napier family sold the manor, it passed through several hands, including, in the 19th century, a Colonel Shrapnel, the inventor of a type of shell that was used in the First World War and which bears his name.

The church is dedicated to St Mary and has a 12th-century chancel arch and west tower which has had some later alteration. The mediaeval font is interesting and unique. It is drum shaped and embellished by an intricately knotted rope decoration and strange carved heads. It sits on top of another font which was originally in the coastal church of St Giles at West Bexington. Invading French forces destroyed the latter church in 1440 and remnants of the font were removed to Puncknowle to act as a base for the one that was currently in situ.

The base of the font.

On the Knoll, the steep hill above the village, are three bowl barrows. Two have been partially excavated and various archaeological remains found. In the 1890s, a Frederick Cheney and his father found a Bronze Age urn containing a human jaw fragment in the flattened barrow that supports the Revenue Hut on the southern side of the mound, which had been exposed by the burrowing of rabbits. Also in this barrow a cinerary urn was found in 1908. The whole was sealed by a slab capstone. The northern barrow had been disturbed in the mediaeval period, leaving just fragments of urn and cremated bone.

The Knoll, seen from the B3157 coast road.

In 1791 a farm labourer discovered a huge hoard of coins in the area, numbering well over a thousand. Time had played a rough hand with this treasure trove, for most of the coins were hardly decipherable and much decayed, rending them almost worthless.

The Grade II listed building that sits on top of one of the barrows appears to be a shepherd's hut but is in fact a late 18th-century look-out and signal station with a small later extension. It has also been used as a tiny coastguard's cottage, known as the Revenue Hut.

Revenue Hut atop the Knoll.

Smuggling, particularly of liquor, was a more or less constant activity along this stretch of coast and this building, acting as a look-out, must have been a deterrent to this activity. The hut also had another use because of its far-reaching views over most of Lyme Bay. If the herring or mackerel were shoaling they would have been seen from here. A tell-tale sign of large shoals of fish was the frenzied activities of gulls and this would have alerted the look-out, who would then hasten to let the locals know that a huge piscatorial bounty was heading their way.

A good vantage point.

There was a Romano-British settlement at Puncknowle. Remains discovered in a field called 'Walls' 500 m east of the Knoll were thought to be that of a religious complex, consisting of an enclosure and surrounding masonry buildings, dating from the second half of the 4th century, with a temple, which was excavated between 1989 and 1991. All that can be seen now are a few rises and falls within the field.

Puncknowle is an intriguing village of handsome stone cottages and farm buildings. It is set in a landscape that alternates between hills and downland and the nearby swell of the sea, with the Knoll serving as a landmark for mariners for centuries.

RAMPISHAM
Ancient Crosses and an Old Bridge

OS maps: Explorer 117 or Landranger 194

Grid refs: Church ST562023, Broom Hill wayside cross ST564026

Directions: Take the A356 north-east from Maiden Newton for approx. 3 miles, until you see the large aerial masts on your left. At the crossroads turn right to Rampisham and drive down the hill. After 1 mile you pass the church on your right. Park shortly after this, near the crossroads. To the right is a bridleway leading to the old bridge, hidden in the trees. To see the roadside cross, walk up the road north towards Evershot and it is on your right after approx. 400 m.

Rampisham is mentioned in the *Domesday Book* of 1086. In those times the settlement was known as 'Ramesham'. There are said to be the remains of two probable prehistoric mounds about a mile from the church. Any history of these has been hard to find, as is any knowledge of a standing stone that was once in the area but whose location is now a mystery.

In Broom Hill, a wayside cross dating from the 15th century stands on the grassy verge near to what used to be the old rectory. This could be the cross that once stood on the village green, outside a now disappeared pub called the Tiger's Head, having been moved to its present position at the beginning of the 19th century. What remains of the shaft bears worn-away carvings, with one

Remains of ancient crosses in the village of Rampisham.

faint figure thought to be that of St Michael. Another fragment of a cross up the road was found buried in a garden in the village.

There is another much larger cross in the churchyard. This is the remains of an early 16th-century cross, constructed of hamstone. Approximately a third of the cross remains, with detailed but worn carving said to represent the

martyrdom of Saints Stephen and Edmund and Archbishop Thomas à Becket. On the other side of the cross are depictions of two crowned figures seated at a table, a man kneeling, St Peter and various monks, fools and two men in armour. A stone-stepped pedestal supports what is left of the cross. The date inscribed on it is 1516; also the words *Fili Dei misereri mei et sic Porter in nomini thu Amen MDXVI*, the translation of

Stepped cross in the churchyard.

which is 'Oh Son of God have mercy upon me and thus says Porter in thy name. Amen'. The person called Porter died in 1516 and little is known of his history.

The church is dedicated to St Michael and All Saints, and a parish church has stood on this site for over 700 years. The oldest part still standing is the tower, which is built on the south side of the church and largely dates from 1326. It used to contain a chantry chapel in memory of the son of the lady of the manor. The belfry was added in 1858. The main body of the church is Victorian and was rebuilt in two stages: the first design was largely the work of Augustus Pugin, whose somewhat florid designs were vastly influential. He designed a new east window and chancel. Thomas Hardy was likely to have been involved in the later restoration as he was at that time an architectural assistant to John Hicks, a local architect from Dorchester. Hicks extended the tower and rebuilt the nave.

A Roman pavement was found about a mile north-north-west of the church on common land in 1799. It measured 4×3 m and was apparently in good condition. The patterning was intricately composed of tesserae about 5cm^2 and the decoration consisted of a broad border surrounding a large 12-petalled floral ornamentation overlaying a striped pattern of concentric rings, with striped quadrants at each corner. Sadly this rare piece of our history was smashed by treasure-seekers, a situation echoed by the destruction of the Roman pavement found in Halstock in the 19th century by those also looking for treasure – a hypothetical treasure which was never found.

The village is set in a wooded valley through which runs a tributary of the

River Frome. Over this small river spans an old bridge. Built of stone, it has two spans plus a later extension which is a slightly smaller arch. The two original arches are thought to date from the late 16th/early 17th century. The bridge is a memorable addition to the locality and has been at the hub of village life for centuries. Now it is by-passed and has become a foot bridge of quiet seclusion.

All the pack ponies, driven beasts, carts and people that historically used the bridge over the centuries are now just faint memories.

As one stands on the bridge, looking into the clarity of the water below, the continuum of movement puts one in a timeless moment. The beauty of ever-flowing water is that it manifests one of the mysteries of the life-force in an accessible way. Water, in the form of springs, rivers and lakes, was seen as holy in prehistoric and early historic times and was viewed as a receptacle of vast spiritual potency.

The River Frome flows under the old bridge.

On a more mundane level, apart from providing water for physical needs, rivers freshen the energy around where they flow and this is beneficial to those who live in the vicinity. The flowing waters act as a conduit, taking away stagnant airs and energies and subtly refreshing the environment. To use a Chinese term, the *chi* or life-force of the area is enriched by clean oxygenating water and this is of benefit to all.

SOUTH PERROTT
Mohun Castle, Moats and a Neolithic Ritual Site

OS maps: Explorer 116 or Landranger 193

Grid refs: Church and Mohun Castle ST472068, Moat ST473084, Pickett Farm ST472054

Directions: South Perrott straddles the A356, 3 miles south-west of Crewkerne, close to the Somerset border. There is a small parking area in the middle of the village opposite the pub. The church is just off the main road and the churchyard gives the best view of the former Mohun Castle site. To view the moat, drive or walk north up Pipplepen Lane. Park just after Pipplepen Farm and take the footpath on the right signposted North Perrott. Just over the railway line, the path skirts the eastern edge of a dense clump of trees which has completely enveloped the moat. Pickett Farm is 2 miles south of South Perrott, down Picket Lane, but the archaeological site is on private land and therefore not accessible.

The River Parrett Trail goes through South Perrott.

South Perrott at one time was probably a place of some importance but now is just a small village bisected by a busy road. The name Perrott comes from the River Parrett, which rises at nearby Chedington. The river flows north-west through Somerset and enters the sea at Bridgwater Bay National Nature Reserve near Burnham-on-Sea on the Bristol Channel.

Mohun Castle was originally a fortified manor but now only survives as traces of rectangular moat, of which part has been absorbed into the churchyard. The manor house, glorified by the description of 'castle', was

Remains of Mohun Castle – a geophysical survey discovered various buried wall footings and a possible drainage system.

dismantled during the 17th century and very little of anything visible now remains.

William de Mohun was granted lands at Dunster in Somerset by William the Conqueror. The surname was taken from Moyon near Saint-Lo in Brittany. De Mohun was a person of importance and William the Conqueror assigned to him 56 manors in Somerset, 11 in Dorset, one in Devon and one in Wiltshire. There were Mohuns at Fleet by Chesil Beach.

Moated sites such as this, which have a rectangular ditch, normally indicate a defensive structure built for a reasonably important building. Another moat lies 1 mile north, just off Pipplepen Lane towards North Perrott. Documentary evidence suggests the site was the medieval mansion residence of the De Pipplepens. Various moats still survive in West Dorset, including one surrounding Corscombe Court and others at Benville and Batcombe, and there are around 6,000 moated sites known in England.

The moat south of North Perrott is an irregular diamond shape, approx. 80 m long by 75 m wide, and surrounded by bushes and trees.

Moats are intriguing structures because in many examples the function is perfectly understandable, but in other cases it is not so clear and is more of a mystery. Moats surrounding castles or manor houses are defensive structures, designed to deter raiders from gaining access to the main building. However, in some situations this is not so obviously the case. There are some moats where the central island is too small to be the site of a manor. The question is raised as to what purpose these types of moat have.

Ponds are sometimes built by wildfowlers as an attraction for ducks and other semi-aquatic wild birds, but not even the keenest and most avid of wildfowlers would go to the trouble of building a fairly large moat and island.

It is possible that some moats stem from late prehistoric times and that they served a ritual purpose of some kind, an example being lunar celebrations of some sort, the moon being reflected in the water. They would be clear of the trees and vegetation that now surround most moats and on a full moon the water surrounding the island would be silvered.

There were moats in ancient Egypt and in the ruins of Babylon, moats in Africa and Japan. Probably most of these were constructed for defensive purposes, but there is always the possibility that some might have been constructed for religious ceremonies. Water has been seen as a living emblem of the spiritual principle of life, fluid and reflective and essential for survival. To be surrounded by this quality could give a sense of sanctification, similar to the holy quality that certain islands possess.

There are various sacred islands in Britain, such as Iona on the Scottish coast, and in Wales, Anglesey, the sacred isle of the druids, and Bardsey Island, the place of saints. The Otherworld has sometimes been described as located on an island. The island created by a moat could be a place that was 'other', where no human would go, a place set aside as the abode of spirits, surrounded by water that in the clear night skies reflected the shimmering opalescence of moonlight.

Speaking to a local Somerset archaeologist, my ideas were received with a certain degree of interest, but until there are archaeological digs in and around certain moats there will always be some that are an enigma.

Another interesting feature in the South Perrot vicinity is Pickett Farm, situated about a mile south of the village along ancient Picket Lane and one of the oldest farms in the area. The partially 15th-century farmhouse is set back from the lane. The building has a 17th-century core and retains a 15th-century east wing. Here can be found an original traceried window. Approximately 30 years ago, the Legg family took over the farm. They had consistently found one particular field difficult to plough, with rocks and oddments, such as roof tiles and pottery shards, obstructing the ploughing. They invited Tony Robinson and the 'Time Team' to investigate the area. This investigation proved rewarding.

The land surrounding the farm is of particular archaeological interest, though unfortunately none of this is accessible to the public. An initial field-walking exercise discovered small quantities of prehistoric worked flint, Roman and mediaeval pottery shards, and post-mediaeval pottery and building materials. A small amount of Roman coins was found by metal detecting.

A geophysical survey discovered a mound within an oval enclosure. Further investigation found that this structure was Late Neolithic and it had probably been a base for ritual activity into the Early Bronze Age and beyond. This monument is close to a watershed and the sources of two rivers, a typical geographic site for religious activity of that time. Bronze Age pottery was also found in the area. The ring ditch and mound, after detailed excavation, was seen to be the basis of a prehistoric ritual burial site, dating from around 4000 BC. In later times, 2500–1600 BC, the site became a funerary Bronze Age mound, possibly surrounded by a timber circle.

The Roman period also revealed ritual activity here, with votive offerings of coins, discovered on the eastern side of the site, and a few others discovered in shallow scoops. It seems that the site was venerated probably into mediaeval times. This would imply that this site, unknown for hundreds of years and long forgotten, was hugely important for thousands of years, from the Neolithic through to the Bronze Age, Iron Age, Roman times and beyond. No post-mediaeval artefacts have been found and presumably it was with Christianity that beliefs started to change and slowly the old pagan sites began to lose their value within the local and wider communities. The pilgrims started to drop away, the old gods were forgotten and, with the advent of the plough, many of the prehistoric sites became hidden. What was once sacred became lost under pastureland and crops. Who knows what still lies hidden?

STANTON ST GABRIEL
A Ruined Church and Fae Wood

OS maps: Explorer 116 or Landranger 193

Grid refs: Langdon Hill NT car park SY413931, Church SY402924

Directions: Take the A35 west from Bridport for approx. 3 miles, and at the top of the
steep hill after Chideock take the first turning left (if you reach the Farm Shop you
have missed the unmarked turn). Follow Muddyford Lane for 50 m, then turn left
again down Langdon Lane to Langdon Hill NT car park. Take the footpath south
around the base of the hill, through the wood, then follow the sign towards Golden
Cap. After a short distance across an open field, bear right on the footpath to St
Gabriel's. The church is approx. 500 m further on, down the hill. To return, continue
downhill and start to take the lane away from the holiday cottages. Immediately
on your right is a footpath along the stream, past ponds and through St Gabriel's
Wood, which eventually brings you back to the west side of Langdon Hill.
Walk around the north side for the shortest distance back to the car park.

The village of Stanton St Gabriel (Stantone being Old English for 'farm on
stoney ground') was once the site of a Saxon settlement, recorded in the
Domesday Book. 'Stantone' was the original name of the settlement, St Gabriel
being added later. The surrounding land would have been divided up into
smallholdings, and remnants of these can faintly be seen, along with old paths

Approaching Stanton St Gabriel from Langdon Hill.

and traces of ancient fields and hedgerows. All that remains now is a large thatched farmhouse, transformed into four holiday cottages, together with a small cob cottage and the ruins of the church of St Gabriel.

The church was formerly a chapel of ease for nearby Whitchurch Canonicorum during the Middle Ages. During this period the musical instruments used in the services were brought by the small church band over the fields, with the parson accompanying them, astride his horse. The earliest known reference to it is 1240, when it was known as the parish church. However, by the early 16th century the small community was hard-pressed to find the funds to keep the building dry and waterproof. The exposed position and extreme vicissitudes of maritime weather, coupled with a diminishing population, eventually rendered the church untenable and it slipped into inevitable decline. By the end of the 18th century the church was only occasionally used.

Holy Communion is still celebrated at this little church on Ascension Day.

The situation was not helped by the road being downgraded. At one time the main coastal route between Bridport and Charmouth used to pass through here. Eventually, due to its exposed position, the old road proved too costly to maintain and a new road was built to the north through Morcombelake. After this, what was left of the populace at Stanton St Gabriel largely moved away. Fishing and farming had formed the basis of habitation here, but coastal erosion led to difficulties in gaining access to the sea and also diminished farmland. The hamlet imploded, with many people finding work in the mills and ropewalks of Bridport.

A haven for smugglers.

The old church became totally disused and instead served a purpose as a receptacle for local smugglers' tobacco, French silk and kegs of brandy. Smugglers would come ashore of a night and, dragging their booty up the rough cliff path, would hide it in the sanctified recesses of the isolated disused church until it could be safely distributed.

There is a sad, if possibly apocryphal story for the founding of the church. A recently wedded couple were caught out at sea in a vicious storm. Escaping from the stricken ship in a small boat, they battled through the waves in an attempt to come ashore. The young husband, Bertram, prayed to St Gabriel to save their lives and vowed to build a church near wherever they landed on shore. For two days they battled the storm until eventually they were washed up on the beach, but although Bertram survived, his wife died in his arms. However, being true to his word, he had the church built and dedicated to St Gabriel.

In 1841 a new church, also dedicated to St Gabriel, was built at Morcombelake and in 1883 some parts of the old chapel were installed in the new church. This added a certain charm to the new building. The old rood beam, dating from 1500, and font were removed to the new church. In 1960 a field trip to the ruined chapel found amongst the rubble two 15th-century corbels carved as a man and a woman. It is possible that these depict Bertram and his wife, and for safe-keeping they are now stored in the Dorset County Museum.

Nearby to Stanton St Gabriel is St Gabriel's Wood. This is a small, compact wood which is owned by the National Trust. It contains a good mixture of native hardwood and has the unspoilt feel of ancient woodland.

In the old days, woods held a fascination for people. There were far more forested areas and huge swathes of countryside were covered with trees. Travelling through these arboreal fastnesses could sometimes be unsettling, particularly when other beings were also abroad. The woods of Yellowham Hill near Dorchester were reputed to be inhabited by Woodwoses, hairy humanoid creatures in the mould of the American Bigfoot. It would be easy

In spring and summer St Gabriel's Wood is awash with wildflowers and is a perfect example of an old-fashioned wood that has been largely left alone.

to scoff at what could be considered ignorant fanciful superstition if it wasn't for an occurrence at Stourhead that was recounted to me a couple of years ago.

A friend of mine who works at Stourhead was approached by an Italian man who had been walking in the gardens and seemed disturbed and ill at ease. He asked her if ghostly things were ever reported, and she answered that things have sometimes been sensed in the house but not particularly in the gardens. It seemed that the man and his girlfriend were photographing trees just beyond the Lily Lake, at the edge of the gardens. Suddenly, off the path to the right, near where the tallest oak in the park is, they saw a black substantial shape moving fast between the trees and finally disappearing up the incline. The man assured my friend that this creature was no illusion but very real indeed. My friend mentioned to him that a black panther had been seen near Alfred's Tower which is less than a mile away, but he told her what he had seen was not four legged but two. He had definitely seen something, as had his girlfriend, and they were disturbed because there was no rational explanation for what this was. We have lost our vocabulary for this sort of sighting and thus it has no quantifiable reality. But if we bring the imaginative faculty into play, then what these two people saw matches the description of a Woodwose, or the Wiltshire equivalent – a Wildman, a strange elemental force of nature that inhabits a parallel world that sometimes melds into ours.

A parallel could possibly exist at St Gabriel's Wood. On the western edge there is a meadow with a pond and the area sparkles with dragonflies and marsh-loving flowers such as yellow flag irises. A 'sensitive' person that I know, who holds down a high-powered job and is in no way overwhimsical, feels that this area, including the wood, is 'fae', a fairy place.

Why would a wood be thought of as a fairy wood? What makes it different from other woods, and what, or who, are fairies? There are no easy answers. They feature in literature and poetry, viz *A Midsummer Night's Dream* and the poem 'Tam Lin' and many other literary works. Fairies do not necessarily sport green tights and jerkins, gauzy dresses and wings; they are shape shifters and could appear as normal yet a bit odd, such as having red eyes, as had an unearthly woman and child seen in the dusk not many years ago by a farmhand in a field above Beaminster.

Some places just have a different 'feel' to them. The imagination and senses are stimulated and implicated in this, but the rational mind is not. There are fairy traditions in much of Britain and in most world cultures. Various places have fairy connotations, such as Fairy Toot long barrow near Butcombe in Somerset and the Music Barrow at Bincombe (see the chapter on Bincombe), and many ancient sites such as hillforts, stone circles and standing stones seem to attract them. To many they seem more a part of our ancient folk history and have no relevance to modern life. They are part of countryside blather and folklore, completely out of kilter with today. Yet they cannot be completely dismissed. They are that aspect of 'the strange' that rarely intrudes into modern life. They are of that race of beings that includes the Wildman and Bigfoot. They are traditionally associated with the natural world – the countryside and specific features within it, such as woods, moorland, hills and mountains and other areas where nature has been untrammelled by humans. The part they play in our lives is difficult to quantify; it is negligible because most of us do not believe in them, but if we did believe or at least not totally dismiss, there might be a door opened that would give us an enhanced appreciation of some of the inner workings of the landscape – a picture that did not necessarily have pixies sitting on toadstools but had birds whose song was a little bit sweeter, leaves on trees that danced when there was no breeze, gurgling rivers that had the sound of a melody.

Fairy litany is a strange mix, an archaic substructure seemingly melded with imaginative whimsy. Yet despite this, fairyland is embedded in our folklore and, although having lost its vibrancy in a disbelieving world, this strange place with its unearthly denizens cannot totally disappear; only our ability to comprehend and have some sort of understanding of it can.

STOCKWOOD
A Hermit's Church

OS maps: Explorer 117 or Landranger 194

Grid refs: Roadside parking ST587071, Church ST590069

Directions: Stockwood is approx. 14 miles north of Dorchester, just off the A37 Yeovil road. Take the turn for Chetnole, and you soon enter Stockwood. Take the lane to Church Farm and park respectfully, as it is a working farm. The church is tucked away but clearly signed, with a footpath leading across the field to your left.

Stockwood lies in a secluded wooded setting under the north-western slopes of Bubb Down. Nestled within this tranquillity next to a 17th-century farmhouse, Church Farm, lies St Edwold's church, which measures only 9×3.5 m, making it one of the tiniest churches in England.

Stockwood, a secluded spot.

It is thought to be originally of Saxon construction and would have been a single cell. It was rebuilt in the early 15th century, with windows consisting of trefoiled lights with tracery. There is a 17th-century altar table and the

Georgian bell tower atop the church containing one small bell.

west porch was added around this time, as was the interesting bell turret. More building and restoration work was undertaken in the 17th century, work that is remembered by the date '1636' inscribed on the porch. New pews added in the late 19th century replaced earlier ones.

There are just a few gravestones in the tiny churchyard, marking the graves of ten people who died in the 18th and 19th centuries. There is the sense that this is a place locked away in some sort of historical bubble, preserving a certain solitude that divorces it from modern life. That is not to say that this church is redundant in the sense that it has no further use, more that it is in a way rarefied and thus immune from the grosser ramifications of every-day life. The church was declared redundant on 23 January 1959 and ceded to the Churches Conservation Trust on 1 March 1972. Very occasional services are held.

Edwold was the far lesser known brother of St Edmund the Martyr, King of East Anglia. Edwold had a hermit's cell at Cerne Abbas as well as the cell here at Stockwood. Edmund was killed by the Danes under Ivar the Boneless in 870, and Edwold was offered the crown but declined. As a hermit, he led the life of a man dedicated to his faith. When he died he was buried at Cerne Abbas. With the rebuilding of the monastery in 987 his bones were thought to have been re-interred in the monastic chapel.

The original name for Stockwood was Stoke St Edwold. The saint chose this site for his cell because it fitted his ideal as a place for worship and contemplation. Secluded from the mainspring of life by its position within a wooded combe, it must have spoken to this early saint as a place of sanctuary and peace.

Anglo-Saxon saints date from the onset of Christianity in Britain. They were active from approximately AD 600 up to the Norman Conquest in 1066. Both Eadwold (the original Saxon name of St Edwold) of Cerne and Stockwood and Juthwara (St Juthware) of Halstock and Sherborne lived in Dumnonia, the sub-Roman name for this part of Dorset. These early saints, bringing with them the beginnings of Christianity in Britain, were hardy characters who

Inside St Edwold's.

valued a certain amount of hardship as a refining mechanism for the soul. The Christianity they introduced was known as Celtic, and before the onset of the Church of Rome, this Christianity was fresher, more natural and simplistic and had a certain raw appeal. The saints practised what they preached and led, for the most part, exemplary lives of devotion and charitable acts, giving to the communities around them a glimpse of the core of their religion.

This little church of St Edwold carries memories of those times when religion had a greater simplicity and was accessible to all members of the community. The early saints were bringing with them not only a different belief system and spirituality but also a different way of acting within society. People were given a template of how to behave, which some could say was constrictive. However, the main opinion seemed to be acceptance of the fact that it was helpful to have a direction that allowed people to accord with others in ways that are beneficial and harmless. The guise of spirituality changes with the times and gives rise to the old adage that people get the religion they deserve. Whatever salutes spiritual freedom and recognises the good in people and life is probably beyond definition of the term 'religion'.

STONEBARROW HILL
Old Ways and Smugglers' Paths

OS maps: Explorer 116 or Landranger 193

Grid ref: National Trust car park SY382933

Directions: Stonebarrow Hill is immediately east of Charmouth, off the A35. Just south of Newlands Holiday Park, turn left up the steep and narrow Stonebarrow Lane – be prepared for vehicles approaching. Drive up to the top of the hill where there is an NT car park, toilets and small shop.

Stonebarrow Hill rises to a height of 148 m and there are 25 miles of footpaths in this area known as the Golden Cap Estate. Looking east there is the great curve of Chesil Beach and Portland in the distance, and to the west on a clear day you might even see Dartmoor.

The cliff face below Stonebarrow Hill, part of which is known as Cain's Folly, is unstable and often brings fossils down to the beach in frequent rock falls. These cliffs were formed during the Jurassic Age, and the further east one travels, the younger they are. An example of the Middle Jurassic period is seen at Golden Cap, the highest point on the south coast of England.

The lower section of the cliffs is known as the Belemnite Marls. Belemnites were a kind of primitive squid, possessing ten arms armed with small hooks used for grasping prey. These strange creatures had hard internal skeletons ending in a bullet-shaped rostrum, which is normally the main part of the fossilised remains. Very few fossils are found that preserve the soft parts of these creatures, but when they are discovered it can be seen that they possessed an ink sac. They also had beaks, tail fins and large eyes and so were similar to modern squids in many ways.

A little higher up the cliffs is an area known as the Green Ammonite beds where fossils of ammonites are often revealed. Ammonites were a class of marine invertebrate related to squid, octopuses and cuttlefish. They are a shelled nautilus species, similar to those still alive today. Their name was suggested by the Greek philosopher Pliny the Elder who

Stonebarrow Hill is a great starting point for miles of footpaths around the Golden Cap estate.

died in AD 79. He called them *Ammonis cornua* (horns of Ammon) because the Egyptian god Ammon was normally depicted with ram's horns.

Stonebarrow has a large amount of heathland and flower-filled meadows interspersed with wooded copses on the slopes. Many butterflies can be seen in summer including Green Hairstreak, Common Blue, Dark Green Fritillary and Silver-washed Fritillary. Peregrine falcons sometimes soar along the western cliff tops, along with the occasional raven. The ancient landscape of trackways, hedgerows and fields found here is a product of many centuries of traditional farming, which encourages wildlife. The uncut meadows are a haven for deer, rabbits, birds and insects.

Many paths criss-cross the hill, and in the past it is highly probable that some were used by smugglers, carrying their barrels of brandy and other fine commodities. Smuggling, as stated in an earlier chapter, was endemic in Dorset. The network of paths found on Stonebarrow, some so ancient as to be prehistoric, would be difficult to fully explore and the excisemen must have been confounded on many an occasion.

Westhay Farm on Stonebarrow was once part of a mediaeval settlement and is now owned by the National Trust. The term 'hay' is common in Dorset and means an enclosure. Nearby is a small area of woodland known as Monument Copse, which marks the spot where the local squire, Robert Hilliard, died in 1876.

This lovely hill is attractive to walkers and, despite the awkward approach, has much parking. However, because of the myriad paths here one can be alone

Stonebarrow can absorb many people and there is seldom the sense of intrusion to obscure one's appreciation of the stupendous landscape on display.

very quickly. These old paths have been traversed for centuries by country people going about their business. The idea of walking for leisure would be a rarity to many in the past, but now the situation is reversed and walking is seen as stimulating and healthful. Walking up here on Stonebarrow can produce not only health for the body but peace for the mind.

The view east to Golden Cap

SYDLING ST NICHOLAS
An Ancient Settlement
and the Belling Stone

OS maps: Explorer 117 or Landranger 194

Grid refs: Church and Cross village parking SY632994, Belling Stone roadside parking ST647002, Belling Stone ST646008

Directions: Take the A37 north from Dorchester for approx. 4 miles. As you leave Grimstone, turn right under the viaduct for Sydling. This is a pleasant road alongside the Sydling Water stream and past several watercress beds. The church and cross are in the centre of the village on the left. Park near the bus shelter opposite the village hall. For the stone, drive north out of the village and bear right at the fork. Turn right at the T-junction next to the ford, taking the road up towards Cerne Abbas. Near the top of the hill park opposite the entrance to Higher City Farm. Walk about 600 m north to the stone, and just before the dog-leg in the track the stone is set into the hedge. Just south of Sydling, a footpath heads south-east through Huish Farm and up Shearplace Hill, where some early settlement remains can be seen.

'Sydling' means 'large ridge'. Sydling St Nicholas was once owned by the Elizabethan minister Sir Francis Walsingham. It is rumoured that in the great tithe barn close to the church there is a beam carved with the initials of Lady Ursula Walsingham, I.U.W. 1590. This barn can still be viewed from the churchyard.

The roof is now constructed from corrugated iron, but the walls seem sturdy and it appears the barn has not yet outlived its usefulness.

One of the gargoyles on the roof near the south door featured in the 1967 film Far from the Madding Crowd, *drenching poor Fanny Robin's grave.*

In the centre of the village by the crossroads are the remains of the shaft and pedestal of a cross thought to date from the 15th century. There used to be a large ancient elm shading the cross, but it was blown down in 1880. The road behind to the left leads up to the church of St Nicholas. This was founded in 983, but the present building is a mixture of elements dating from the 15th to the 19th century. There is also a 12th-century font and some fine-quality family monuments in the church.

There has been a settlement in and around the valley for almost 5000 years, but the present shape of the village is largely derived from Saxon occupation. In 1936 two Neolithic hand axes were found on land belonging to Magiston Farm. A Bronze-Age settlement dating from 1600–1200 BC is sited on Shearplace Hill, south-east of the village. Post holes suggest that there were three stages of development in the construction of this site, according to excavations undertaken there in 1958. A timber roundhouse was the first structure, later replaced by a palisade surrounding two houses. This small complex was enclosed by a protective bank and ditch. The final stage of the settlement was the replacement of the original dwellings by two houses. These have left traces that confirm that the westerly building was 8.2 m in diameter, the other

The stream running through the village is Sydling Water, a tributary of the River Frome.

building being smaller and less discernible. These two sites can be seen as rounded depressions, separated by a low bank with traces of an enclosing bank. A Celtic field system surrounds this homestead and a path leads north to a major trackway, the Wessex Ridgeway. There are two barrows, not easily seen, situated a couple of hundred metres south towards the barns.

About 1 mile north, near the hamlet of Up Sydling, there are three bowl barrows on Cross Hill and four on East Hill, with single barrows dotted around the area. In fact, this area must have been a centre for early activity as there are other Celtic fields on Peak End Hill, a prehistoric village at Buckland Down and traces of Saxon strip farming at Sherrins Farm.

Perched on a ridge to the north-east of Sydling is a gnarled old standing stone in the hedgerow. Apparently the family that live in the nearby farm come to this stone, probably in the early hours of a morning or in the evening dusk, and make a wish. They see it as special and it has become a wishing stone and perhaps local legend has always had it this way. This old Dorset family is keeping up the tradition. This stone does have a sentinel-like quality, perhaps as a guardian of the ways.

The Belling Stone above Sydling St Nicholas.

These ancient singular stones that are dotted around the landscape of Britain normally date from the early Bronze Age. They are an important feature of our landscape because they act as a testament to a time when all the aspects of nature were seen as alive with an energy and spiritual nous that could be quantified. They were, in all likelihood, seen as 'beings', entities that played a part in the identity and spirit of a place.

TRENT
A Legendary Pool and Crop Circle

OS maps: Explorer 129 or Landranger 183

Grid refs: Roadside parking ST590186, Barrow (entrance) ST609189

Directions: From Yeovil take the A30 towards Sherborne and after 1 mile turn left
towards Over Compton. Trent is approx. 2 miles beyond Over Compton. Parking
is available on the road near the church and at the village hall. In addition to the
church, the village is attractive and worth exploring on foot. Permissive access
to Trent Barrow is only possible from the north off Ham Lane, and only between
1 March and 31 August. Ham Lane is narrow and has no parking. Walk to the
beautifully kept village pond at the eastern end of the village, then bear north-east
up Ham Lane for about 0.5 miles. The entrance to Trent Barrow is on your right.
The estate and much of the village is owned and managed by the Ernest
Cook Trust (www.ernestcooktrust.org.uk).

Trent Barrow is a small but distinctive wooded hill to the east of the village. At
the top of this hill is a horseshoe-shaped earthwork surrounding a medium-
sized pool that is said to be bottomless. Local legend states that a coach and
horses once plunged into this pool and disappeared, leaving naught but ripples
as evidence of a tragic misadventure. It is claimed that on moonlit nights the
sound of ghostly galloping horses and wailing voices can be heard. There is a
similar story about another spectral coach and horses that haunts the Roman
road that crosses the River Frome near Muckleford. The coach overturned into
a bog and the driver and horses were killed. On wild nights, when the moon is
a-gleam, the horse-beats can be heard, thudding like some forgotten portent.

Trent Barrow.

Disappearing coach and horses, into an either watery or boggy grave, seems to be a theme in many local folk tales and might allude to the coach and horses as being a metaphor for death or transport into the realm of death. This could be a dim memory of certain rites, where horses and a carriage or cart were sacrificed at the death of a notable member of the tribe, possibly to act as transport to those hidden realms. Or perhaps this is a memory that tells of an actual accident.

There are similar legends attached to pools near Leigh (possibly just north of Frampton Farm), a village about 8 miles south of Trent, where, again, a coach and horses plus four headless women haunt the area. At Stinsford near Dorchester there is another tale of a like nature, with a coach and horses plunging headlong into a 'bottomless' pool lying south of the village and formed from a tributary of the River Frome.

The pool on Trent Barrow.

The pool at Trent also features in an old legend, equally dramatic as the ghost story but with added mystical overtones. Trent Barrow is part of a small range of hills which culminate at Cadbury Castle. It is Cadbury that gives the clue to the legend linked to Trent pool. Many believe that the sacred sword Excalibur, forever part of British mythic history with King Arthur, was flung into Dozmary Pool on Bodmin Moor in Cornwall. However, the pool above Trent is also a contender. Here is another possible last resting place for the magical and emblematic sword, a sword that is so deeply connected with British myth and rites of kingship. Perhaps it was here, not Dozmary, that Sir Bedivere threw Excalibur into the water, recognising this pool as a portal to the Otherworld. The pool and the surrounding woodland does have a feeling of mystery. But the legendary status regarding Excalibur is little known.

Another king is linked with Trent. Charles II took refuge in Trent Manor in 1651. At that time the manor was owned by Colonel Wyndham who was a Royalist sympathiser. After the disastrous Battle of Worcester, fought on 3 September 1651, the King had to go into hiding. He arrived in Trent, dressed as a servant, on 17 September. Once safely in the manor, he hid out in Lady Anne Wyndham's room, which, in case the Parliamentarians came looking for him, had a hiding place under the roof. He stayed at Trent for over 2 weeks and when he was finally restored to the throne rewarded Colonel Wyndham by giving him £1000 and a pension of £600 and ennobled him with a baronetcy.

Trent church, dedicated to St Andrew, stands in a lovely churchyard which contains the steps and shaft of an ancient cross. Inside the church are some curiously carved bench ends, an ancient intricately carved rood screen, a

richly carved late 17th-century Flemish pulpit, some helmets and gauntlets hanging on the walls and some fine manorial altar tombs. The north transept is laid out as a display area, and includes a beautiful coffin cart. There are also tombs of varying grandeur belonging to the Phelips family, a member of whom aided Charles II to escape to France. This is also one of the few churches in the county to have a spire.

The ancient priest's house or chantry abuts the churchyard. This interesting building dates from the reign of Henry VI and was endowed in 1428 by a native of Trent, John Franks, who was Master of the Rolls. He died in 1438, having achieved high government office. This was accompanied by the more modest satisfaction of ensuring that the priests based in Trent were comfortably housed in a fine building of singular beauty.

St Andrew's Church is a treasure-trove of artefacts.

The chantry, now a private residence.

There was a crop circle near Trent Barrow in 2010 composed of a series of circles and rings. It is unusual to find one in Dorset as they seem to occur mainly in Wiltshire. Crop circles are interesting phenomena which have intrigued people for years. Some certainly have been made by people, but others defy easy explanation.

A crop circle is a large pattern found mainly in fields where there are crops of wheat, rye or barley. 'Circles' can sometimes be a misnomer because these patterns are not necessarily always circular. They started to be widely reported in the early 1970s and 90% of these were in southern England. A certain number of these early structures were hoaxes, constructed by 'Doug and Dave', Doug Bower and Dave Chorley. They were apparently inspired by the case of a UFO sighted in Australia which had left a large saucer-shaped depression in the grass. Only in 1991 did they 'come out' as it were and admit to making many of the crop circles. The tools they used were simple, a plank of wood, rope and a baseball cap fitted with a loop of wire.

Although many crop circles could be human-made, a small number defy rational explanation. It would seem that 'real' crop circles show a scorch mark on the stalk of the grain, a mark that is about 3 inches from the ground. The stalks are also bent, rather than broken.

There is a report from Great Eversden near Cambridge in 1934 of crop circles seen being actually formed. A woman, Kathleen Skin, wrote to the *Sunday Express*, which printed her statement in August 1990:

> '*I witnessed a corn circle being formed in 1934. I was gazing over a field of corn waiting to be harvested when I heard a crackling like fire and saw a whirlwind in the centre of the field, spinning stalks, seeds and dust into the air for about a hundred or more feet. I found a perfect circle of flattened corn, the stalks interlaced and their ears lying on each other (some even plaited) on the periphery. The circle was hot to the touch. There was nothing to be seen in the sky – no wind, and no sound. Maybe on a windless day, the corn stalks form an electric current which attracts an electric force in the atmosphere, meeting with such pressure that the corn is pressed hard onto the ground in a circular motion. A sort of miniature tornado.*'

Kathleen was 14 at the time and had stopped to talk to a farmer. She witnessed two circles forming. It seems the force was like a whirlwind which, having created one circle, moved off and made a second. These circles were about 4 m in diameter.

There are other reports of crop circles being formed. In Helions Bumpstead, a village situated where the counties of Suffolk, Essex and Cambridgeshire meet, a boy of 10, Paul Germany, working in the harvest fields in 1935, saw a crop circle form. Again there was a whirlwind effect and all the wheat straw pointed in the same direction. The farm workers had seen this phenomenon before and called it the 'Devil's Twists'.

Thus the crop circle phenomenon predates Doug and Dave's efforts by many years. There have been many early crop circles reported, from one in 1880 found in a field near Guildford, Surrey, to some that appeared through several decades, from 1914 to 1956, in Maiden Bradley, Wiltshire, where local farming families had known about the circles through many generations. Another was seen in 1932 at Bow Hill, near Chichester, Sussex; this consisted of four rings in a barley field. There have been various circles mentioned in scattered sites in Britain throughout the first half of the 20th century, right up until the debacle started by Doug and Dave. It would seem that the complex modern crop circles are brash interlopers, with some of dubious origin. However, that does not explain the person who passed a wheat field on her way to Calne to do a small amount of shopping, only to find a complex crop circle in the middle of the field when she passed the area again on her way home. There would not have been time for human agency to have constructed this, so it seems the mystery remains.

UPWEY
Healing Springs and a Wishing Well

OS maps: Explorer OL15 or Landranger 194

Grid refs: Church parking SY660853

Directions: Upwey is just north of Weymouth, on the B3159 Martinstown road. Heading south from Dorchester on the A354 Weymouth Relief Road, Upwey is clearly signed. An alternative and more attractive route is to leave the A354 for Winterborne Monkton and skirt the southern slopes of Maiden Castle, through the village to a T-junction, then turn left over the South Dorset Ridgeway to Upwey. At the Wishing Well, take the small lane to the church and a car park just beyond it. On Sundays the car park is reserved for worshippers. The entrance to the Wishing Well is back past the church at the road junction.

Two springs rise at Upwey, one from the chalk and the other from gravelly greensand. These springs are the originators of the River Wey which rises fully formed from these two sources. This is unusual, as most rivers arise from their springs as small streams, gradually forming into a larger body of water with

The River Wey flows through the village, eventually meeting the sea at Weymouth.

the addition of other springs and field run-offs. This interesting and possibly unique birthing of a river was probably heralded as special in ancient times and it is likely that this place would have been considered as sacred.

The hamlet of Elwell, part of the parish of Upwey, has a healing well. The Saxon root of the name Elwell (Helewill) means 'healing' or 'oracular'. This well is now no more than a spring that rises in a field at the bottom of Ridgeway Hill, situated behind the place where a pub, the Royal Oak, used to stand. It is interesting that there are two healing springs in close vicinity (one in Upwey, the other in Elwell), even though the one at Elwell is now overlooked and is thought to have been diverted into a horse trough.

In the 18th century a water mill was built on the river, a small distance downstream of Upwey Wishing Well. This mill was rebuilt in 1802 and can be seen today behind the building known as Mill House.

Former Upwey Mill was fed by two courses of water.

The church of St Laurence dates from the 13th century. Inside, watermarks, approximately 10 inches high, can be seen on some of the pews; these are the traces left after a flood that occurred in 1955. There had been heavy rainfall up in the hills and the water had rushed down into the village, causing a massive flood. The church contains, among other interesting features, a small amount of ancient oak wainscoting, a carved pulpit from the time of Charles I, and three 17th-century wooden carvings of saints, among them St Peter. The windows on the north aisle, the font and the porch, which has a mediaeval door, are 15th century. Also of note are the English roses on the walls, depicting the white rose of York and the pink of Lancaster, painted in 1485.

The Green Man is represented here by carvings on capitals of the stone pillars. Some are Victorian copies but two are thought to date from the late 13th/ early 14th century: one is distinctively the foliage-disgorging face that typifies the genus, carved by a

Carving of St Peter, holding keys and a book.

The apprentice's Green Man.

master mason; the other was carved by an apprentice who chose to depict him with grapes coming out of his ears.

Life's underlying fecundity is represented by the different styles of this emblematic image. Heads, normally male, are surrounded by leaves, which can also issue from the mouth and other parts of the face. These strange heads date from mediaeval times and can be found on bench ends, misericords, roof bosses and the capitals atop columns. They are found on both ecclesiastical and secular buildings. The motif has many variations and is found in many cultures throughout the world. The image is a symbol of rebirth and represents the cycle of Spring growth. It is interesting that a figure, which in all purposes appears to be pagan, should be so frequently found in churches, abbeys, chapels and cathedrals. The earliest example found so far dates from AD 400 and is from the tomb of St Abre in the church of St Hilaire-le-Grand in Poitiers, France. Somehow the Green Man has been able to survive as a symbol of the pre-Christian reverence and of the vitality of life and Nature.

Among the graves outside the church (to the left of the porch) is a large table-top tomb with a plaque written in Latin to the memory of William Gould. The Goulds held the Manor of Upwey for many years. They were also connected by marriage to the old-established Dorset family the Mohuns, who owned the Manor of Fleet. The Gould family lived in Upwey House, which was the original Manor House of Upwey.

St Laurence's Church.

The Wishing Well at Upwey was a favourite place for King George III to visit. He took a liking to the taste and clarity of the waters which were said to be particularly good for health. A gold cup was kept at a nearby house for His Majesty's use, and this later became the Ascot Gold Cup of the famous horse race.

The unusual quality of the two springs attracted attention and the area became extremely popular and was commercialised. People would obtain a glass of well water from a custodian, drink most of it and then cast the dregs over their left shoulder whilst making a wish. They would then pay the custodian. Refreshment rooms were built in 1907.

Upwey Wishing Well. The arched seating area was built in 1887 to commemorate Queen Victoria's Golden Jubilee.

Well dressing is a custom normally carried out in summer. Using wet wooden boards covered with a mixture of clay, water and salt, a design is etched onto the clay. The picture is then filled in with natural materials – depending on the season, mainly petals, mosses, seed heads, berries and other organic substances. Tissington in Derbyshire is said to be where well dressing originated, in 1349, but the origins of the tradition possibly stem from ancient pagan activities or from the idea of giving thanks for pure water during plague times. Wishing wells are part of the folklore of the British Isles, and spoken wishes at these special wells were thought to be granted. Water was known to have healing powers. This came from the idea that water was emblematic of spirit, that there were deities in certain waters and that springs and wells were sacred. Offerings were made, sometimes of wooden representations of certain gods and goddesses, sometimes of metal objects, such as swords or coins. Wells were thought to have an invisible guardian and a coin thrown into the well to pay the guardian would grant a wish. This has been handed down to us as the coins which are thrown into wishing wells today. In Norse myths there is a well of wisdom, which would grant infinite wisdom but only if you sacrificed something that was very important to you. The god Odin sacrificed his right eye and, in return, received the ability to see the future and also was given the understanding of how and why things must be. The wishing well at Upwey is not, thankfully, so extreme but is a special place, despite a touch of commercialism. The atmosphere of something unique and ageless still pervades this river's birthing place and wishes made here may have the potency to come true.

WADDON and CORTON
Waddon House and
St Bartholomew's Chapel

OS maps: Explorer OL15 or Landranger 194

Grid refs: Waddon House SY620857, Chapel SY636854

Directions: From Portesham, take Winter's Lane eastwards opposite the church. After 1 mile, Waddon House is on your left. Continue for approx. 1.5 miles and take the right turn down to Corton Farm. The farm and chapel are around to the right, and there is space to park, but please ask permission if anyone is around, to avoid intrusion.

Perched on the hillside just east of Portesham is glorious Waddon House, a beautiful example of a medium-sized historic manor house. It was once owned by the powerful Dorset family the Mohuns. Restored in the 17th century by Colonel Bullen Reymes who inherited the manor of Waddon through his wife in 1651, the building was further gentrified in about 1700 by Henry Chafin. This was achieved by facing the whole building in Portland stone. Sadly the house lost a west wing to a fire in 1704. The manor sits directly on the side of the lane and overlooks the fertile country that borders the sea. The building is surprisingly grand for such a rural location and would not look out of place in a city such as Bath.

In the 1967 film version of Thomas Hardy's Far from the Madding Crowd *Waddon House was portrayed as the home of Farmer Boldwood.*

Corton, 'the tun of the cut', consists of a farm with various outbuildings, a small manor house and an ancient chapel dedicated to St Bartholomew. 'Tun' means town or settlement and 'the cut' is a cutting through solid rock which allowed a road through to the sheltered piece of land whereupon the hamlet was founded. The rock here is an outpost of Purbeck marble, surrounded by the chalk that is endemic to this area. This rocky eminence, part of Friar Waddon Hill, provides protection from northern winds, and people have lived on this piece of land since prehistoric times. 'Waddon' is Old English for 'hill of the woad' ('Wad' is woad and 'don' is hill).

In 1765 some skeletons were found buried 18 inches below the surface in a field called 'Higher Ground', probably on the slopes of Friar Waddon Hill. They were buried in a north-east to south-west orientation and were enclosed with flat stones set edgewise, forming simple coffins. There was a row of between seven and eight rough earthenware vessels, black in colour, and two red pottery vessels. These were grave goods of some kind, perhaps containing offerings for use in the Underworld. Probably these remains date from the Late Bronze Age period. There are also four bowl barrows on Friar Waddon Hill.

St Bartholomew's chapel, also known as Corton chapel, is situated on the lower slopes of Friar Waddon Hill and in the close vicinity of the ancient manor located here with surrounding farmyard. The chapel is a simple rectangular building around 12 m in length and in 1087 it was mentioned in *Domesday*. It initially belonged to a cell of the abbey at Abbotsbury – a free chapel, endowed but costing nothing to the parish priests or parishioners. After the passing of the Chantry Act by Edward VI in 1548, the chapel ceased to be used for religious purposes and became part of the farm buildings. Outhouses were built either side of the building and these were used for carpentry, with a workshop for a wheelwright. The chapel was later used for keeping poultry.

The chapel is basically Transitional Norman in structure. The earliest part still visible is the 12th-century south doorway.

It was saved from being permanently relegated as a farm building by its reconsecration in 1897 by the Bishop of Salisbury. The simple building was used for a while as a private chapel, before eventually opening again as a place of worship for all. Services are now held on the second and fourth Sunday of every month.

Apart from a lovely setting which makes visiting this small ecclesiastical building a joy, the chapel is unusual in that it retains a pre-Reformation stone altar. This altar, made of three slabs of Purbeck marble, is undeniably ancient. The flat stones could possibly be prehistoric, marking a grave or religious site, although more likely they are early Saxon. Pre-Reformation altars, such as this one, are extremely rare due to the decree issued in 1550 by Edward VI that all stone altars should be removed from churches and chapels. Somehow this one escaped, perhaps because it had been hidden.

This little chapel is blessed with a verdant outlook overlooking hills and meadows, edged by the distant glimmer of the sea. The white rocky out-crops on the steep-sided hill behind the chapel catch the light and reflect the sun, reminiscent of similar outcrops in Mediterranean countries. The old manor house basks nearby, managing to convey a beauty formed of a medley of different styles and ages. There is no uniformity in the windows, and the diversity, along with the varied characters and styles, betray the chequered history of the building.

Inside the tiny church at Corton, which was originally a free chapel.

WHITCOMBE
A Field Church of William Barnes

OS maps: Explorer OL15 or Landranger 194

Grid refs: Layby parking and Church SY716883

Directions: Whitcombe is about 2 miles south-east of Dorchester, half way to
Broadmayne, beside the busy A352 Wareham road. There is a small parking area
(no more than a pull-in) on the road, almost opposite the church.
Great care should be exercised when crossing the busy road.

The dedication of this church is unknown, but the site of the church has been
in use since Saxon times and the remains of two Saxon crosses can be found in
the interior. King Athelstan, *c* 966, made Whitcombe part of the endowment
of Milton Abbey and in those days the village would have been much larger.

Whitcombe is a field church, reached by a short path across pastureland.
This gives a bucolic feeling, and even though the road is close by, once in the
environs of the church, consciousness of traffic dies away, to be replaced by
the peace this building provides. The church was made redundant in 1971 and
is now cared for by the Churches Conservation Trust. What remains of the
structure dates from the Norman period.

*Poet and parson William Barnes conducted his first service here in 1847 and his last in
1885. The large tree on the left, outside the churchyard wall, is a mecca for snails.*

Inside a plaque records: 'To the Glory of God and to the memory of William Barnes, the preservation of this church was carried out AD 1912'.

The oldest items to be seen in the church are the remains of two 10th-century Anglo-Saxon cross-shafts, on display in the nave. There are also fragments, presumably from these two crosses, in a corner near the font. All the cross fragments have, as part of their patterning, a decorative interlaced carving, possibly representing eternity. The 12th-century nave and 13th-century Purbeck marble font also bear witness to the church's age, as does the large 15th-century wall-painting and fine waggon roof.

Pre-Reformation churches used to be vibrant, with colourful images covering most of the walls. These images, taken from Biblical teachings, helped a largely illiterate congregation to understand the Bible. The paintings showed aspects of both the Old and New Testament. The stories of the gospels acted as a vivid reminder of the tenets of faith. Prior to the Protestant Church supplanting the Catholic, the churches were full of visual reminders in the guise of paintings, carvings, statues and tapestries. Wall paintings and other highly decorative items in churches are now rare. Most disappeared during the Reformation and walls were painted over during that time, as they were seen as Papist idolatry. Whatever was left disappeared during Cromwellian times as they offended the

Puritan sensibility. Any wall painting that might have been left was vulnerable. If not attended to and repainted as necessary, they just faded and flaked off the wall, mouldering with the ravages of time and neglect.

Sometimes the whitewash that had covered so many of these priceless wall paintings served to protect them through the centuries, although not always from the Victorians. The Victorian ethos seemed to be one of uniformity. With a generic ideal as the template, they hacked off most of the whitewashed plaster in order to resurface the walls. Sadly, many of the remaining frescoes were removed also. But some were saved, as church restorers around the 1940s and 1950s started finding beautifully preserved paintings hidden under the plaster – not a huge number, the majority had been long lost, but enough to recognise a distinctly English style. We are lucky that this part of our history has been saved, or at least partially saved, in this small church. The painting found on the walls here depicts St Christopher carrying Christ as a Child. Only the top part has survived more or less in its entirety; the rest is faint and hard to decipher.

Outside near the porch are the 15th-century remains of the shaft and base of a cross. This is close to an interesting cabinet tomb, with a strange face carved at one end over a crossed pick and spade.

Whitcombe church is evocative of the rustic atmosphere of old Dorset, with sheep often grazing the pasture surrounding it.

Between the western churchyard wall and the road is a large tree with many hundreds of snails crammed into its trunk. There are also many snail shells beneath the tree, the whole thing rather like a sort of snail Valhalla.

There is an interesting stone lying against or perhaps into the front right corner of the churchyard wall that could be significant. It is thought to be a standing stone, dating from prehistoric times and no doubt in place here years before the church was built. Other prehistoric items have been found near the church, including five Palaeolithic hand axes. There are many other prehistoric

Ancient stone propping up the wall.

remains in the area and it is possible that the church may be sited on an earlier pagan holy place.

On nearby Whitcombe Hill in 1963 a 27-inch-long Portland stone relief of a bearded man with a belted tunic and flowing coat, complete with a scabbard for a sword, was excavated. He is on horseback, holding a spear and was found near the remains of a Romano-British building dating from the 2nd or 3rd century. The Royal Commission on Historical Monuments thought the piece could be a shrine dedication to a hero god. Perhaps this figure was a protector of hunters or warriors. In a nearby barrow were found the remains of an Iron Age warrior. Strange sounds have been sometimes heard from the barrow, neither voices nor music.

The lost Mediaeval village of Whitcombe was spread out amongst the 14 acres of land which surrounds the church. There are many tumuli in this area, including a rare bank barrow, and earthworks around the immediate area of the church, the most obvious behind the rear churchyard wall. These are the remains of house platforms and closes. There were still cottages, no more than hovels, surviving here up until the 18th century.

Famed Dorset poet William Barnes was rector here and lived nearby in Came Rectory. It is thought that he preached his first and last sermons at Whitcombe church. It is somehow appropriate that this great ruralist should see this unique place as both seminal and final in the delivery of his thoughts on Deity and the human condition. Barnes is buried beneath a Celtic Cross in the nearby churchyard of St Peter, Winterborne Came, to the west, where he was rector for 24 years, between 1862 and 1886.

WYNFORD EAGLE
An Historic Manor House and Strange Tympanum

OS maps: Explorer 117 or Landranger 194

Grid refs: Roadside parking SY584959

Directions: Wynford Eagle is just 1 mile south-west from Maiden Newton. It is best to park near Manor Farm on the left, as the road to the church is narrow, with soft verges. Proceeding on foot uphill past the church, the bridleway to the north affords views down over the valley and manor house, and further on over Toller Fratrum.

The hamlet of Wynford Eagle lies in a valley surrounded by downland. It is thought that the land has been settled continuously since Neolithic times.

The bucolic setting of Wynford Eagle.

There is an unrecorded standing stone situated on the left of the entrance to Manor Farm, just inside the yard. A bridleway runs past and proceeds up the hill. That this sarsen stone is in its original position is unlikely. A 'sensitive' who delved into the history of this settlement thought that the stone may have

been used as an altar in rituals and originally would have been standing by a chambered tomb, presumably a long barrow. Early in the 18th century this stone was probably taken from its position on the hillside and placed in the farmyard.

The fine manor house was once the seat of one of the old West Country families, the Sydenhams. The name 'Eagle' commemorates an earlier family; the village was once in the ownership of the Norman barony of Aquila or Eagle, a family who were originally based at Pevensey Castle in Sussex.

Wynford Eagle was the birthplace of the physician Thomas Sydenham.

The stone in Manor Farm yard – an interesting edifice that adds another layer to the history of Wynford Eagle.

He was the first person to develop and use the ingredients behind many of the medicines of today. The Sydenhams came to the manor of Wynford Eagle in 1544 and Thomas Sydenham was born here in 1624. He took his degree at Oxford, served in the Parliamentary army and eventually practised as a doctor and surgeon in Westminster. Because of his studies and active application of medical science he was recognised as a skilled clinician and as the founder of modern medicine.

The house, modified by William Sydenham in 1630, is an attractive example of a largely 17th-century manor. Sadly, it was lost to the Sydenhams due to the activities of a family member. A grandson

A stone eagle sits atop the gable of the manor.

of William Sydenham put the building up for a private lottery in 1699. He had apparently cheated by coming to a pre-arrangement with a family friend that she would win but sell it back to the family for a pittance. However, she turned the tables on the arrangement and apparently married and then sold the estate to a neighbour.

The title of the First Baron Wynford of Wynford Eagle was created on 5 June 1829 to ennoble William Draper Best, who was MP For Bridport and in 1816 rose to be Attorney-General to the Prince of Wales. He held other high offices, among them that of Deputy Speaker of the House of Lords.

In the mid-19th century, situated south-west of the manor house, part of a Roman pavement was found, with some more uncovered in 1935. It is thought that these remains were part of a Roman villa.

An old church used to stand 500 m to the south of the present church of St Lawrence. The original church, thought to date from the 12th century, was a mediaeval subsidiary chapel of the church of St Basil at nearby Toller Fratrum. The simple church at Toller Fratrum, a hamlet named after the Knights Hospitallers of St John who were based there until the Reformation, is of interest, particularly because of its Late Saxon/Early Norman font. It is difficult to ascertain exactly what is pictured on the font, but there is a strange creature, possibly the Golden Calf, Christ or St Michael, leading souls from Hell and Moses saving the Israelites. There is also a 12th-century sculpture fragment of St Mary Magdalene wiping the feet of Christ with her hair (her head and Christ's foot and lower drapery are visible). Either side of the west door are two mediaeval head-stops. One wonders if the now-vanished original church at Wynford Eagle had similarly interesting features.

The current church at Wynford Eagle was rebuilt in 1842 but retains a 15th-century chancel arch and 13th-century font. However, the most inter-

St Lawrence's Church today.

esting feature, rescued from the vanished original church, is the tympanum beside the door. A tympanum is a vertical triangular space forming the centre of a pediment; the term can also mean a similar space over a door, embellished by a carving. They are relatively rare; an example, dating

The word 'wyvern' is derived from the old Saxon 'wivere' meaning serpent.

from around 1100, can be found over the south door of St George's Church in Fordington, near Dorchester. It shows St George rescuing the Crusaders from the Saracens at the Battle of Dorylaeum. The carvings on the tympanum at Wynford Eagle are of two beasts aggressively facing each other and appearing to be about to do battle. These creatures are mythical beasts known as wyverns, described as winged dragons with barbed tails. They are the emblem of Saxon Wessex.

Wynford Eagle is a gem of varied delights. The downland setting rolls onwards in every direction. The Manor is beautifully positioned within these pastoral hills and somehow exudes the feeling of being a benefactor, but not oppressively so. There is history here, etched everywhere in the fabric of the place. It is a history that combines the land with the people who have lived and worked upon it. The result is an ageless cavalcade of movement – the seasons, human endeavour and the constant subtle changes endemic in the landscape.

The stream that runs through the water meadows here gives a fluidity to the view.

Bibliography

Belloc, Hilaire (1904, 2013) *The Old Road*. Emereo Publishing, Brisbane

Biltcliffe, Gary (2009) *The Spirit of Portland*. Roving Press, Frampton.

Blythe, Ronald (1986) *Divine Landscapes*. Viking, Harmondsworth.

Bord, Janet (2004) *The Traveller's Guide to Fairy Sites*. Gothic Image, Glastonbury.

Bord, Janet and Colin (1976) *The Secret Country*. Book Club Associates, London.

Crowden, James (Introduction) (2007) *Lewesdon Hill, A Poem (1788) by William Crowe*. Flagon Press, Chard.

Cullingford, Cecil N. (1980) *A History of Dorset*. Phillimore, London.

Devereux, Paul (1990) *Places of Power*. Blandford, London.

Devereux, Paul (2007) *Spirit Roads*. Collins and Brown, London.

Doel, Fran and Geoff (2001) *The Green Man in Britain*. Tempus Publishing, Stroud.

Dorset Federation of Women's Institutes (1990) *Hidden Dorset*. Countryside Books, Newbury, and DFWI, Dorchester.

Dorset Historic Churches Trust (1988) *Dorset Churches*. Friary Press, Dorchester.

Downes, Jonathan, Newland, Robert J. and North, Mark J. (2007) *Dark Dorset Tales of Mystery and Wonder*. CFZ, Bideford.

Gibson, Anthony (2011) *With Magic in My Eyes. West Country Literary Landscapes*. Fairfield Books, Bath.

Harpur, Merrily (2008) *Roaring Dorset! Encounters with Big Cats*. Roving Press, Frampton.

Harte, Jeremy (1996) *Cuckoo Pounds and Singing Barrows*. Dorset Natural History and Archaeological Society, Dorchester.

Harte, Jeremy (1998) *Discover Dorset – Legends*. Dovecote Press, Wimborne.

Hinton, D.A. (1998) *Discover Dorset – Saxons and Vikings*. Dovecote Press, Wimborne.

Hippisley-Cox, R. (1914) *The Green Roads of England*. Methuen, London.

Kirk, Rev Robert (1993, 2008) *The Secret Commonwealth of Elves, Fauns and Fairies*. Dover Publications, New York.

Knight, Peter (1996) *Ancient Stones of Dorset*. Power Publications, Ferndown.

Legg, Rodney (1987) *Mysterious Dorset*. Dorset Publishing Company, Wincanton.

Lloyd, Polly (1988) *Legends of Dorset*. Bossiney Books, Bodmin.

Macfarlane, Robert (2008) *Going to Ground: Britain's Holloways*. Orion Magazine, https://orionmagazine.org/article/going-to-ground-britains-holloways/.

Macfarlane, Robert (2012) *The Old Ways*. Hamish Hamilton, London.

Ollard, Richard (1995) *Dorset*. Dovecote Press, Wimborne.

Pennick, Nigel (1996) *Celtic Sacred Landscapes*. Thames and Hudson, London.

Pollard, Andrew and Brawn, Emma (2009) *The Great Trees of Dorset*. Dovecote Press, Wimborne.

Powys, Llewelyn (2003) *Wessex Memories*. The Powys Press, Gloucester.

Putnam, Bill (1998) *Discover Dorset – The Prehistoric Age*. Dovecote Press, Wimborne.

Royal Commission on Historical Monuments (1970) *An Inventory of Historical Monuments in the County of Dorset – Volume Two*. HMSO, London.

Stanier, Peter (2004) *Dorset's Archaeology*. Dorset Books, Tiverton.

Stewart, R.J. (1990) *Robert Kirk – Walker Between Worlds*. Element Books, Shaftesbury.
Stewart, R.J. (1999) *The Living World of Faery*. Mercury Publishing, New York.
Treves, Frederick (1920) *Highways and Byways in Dorset*. Macmillan, London.
Udal, John Symonds (1922) *Dorsetshire Folk-Lore*. Dorset Books.
Yeats, W.B. (2013) *The Book of Fairy and Folk Tales of Ireland*. Bounty Books, London.

Websites

British History Online – www.british-history.ac.uk
Churches Conservation Trust – http://www.visitchurches.org.uk/
Crop circles – oldcropcircles.weebly.com
Dorset Historic Churches Trust – http://www.dorsethistoricchurchestrust.co.uk/
Ernest Cook Trust: outdoor learning charity – http://ernestcooktrust.org.uk/
Megalithic Portal – http://www.megalithic.co.uk/

Hell Lane, North Chideock.

On Stonebarrow Hill.

About the Author

Louise Hodgson has spent most of her life in the West Country and currently lives in West Dorset. Over the years she has walked and explored this part of the county and some of her most intriguing discoveries are in both this book and the preceding volume *Secret Places of West Dorset*, published by Roving Press. Her work has been seen in various periodicals, including *The Literary Review*. Her artwork has been exhibited in the West Country and London. She has appeared on television – on BBC *Points West* and Network 7. She is an accomplished speaker and gives various illustrated talks for many organisations, including Probus and the Women's Institute. She currently runs a tour company called *Secret Landscape Tours*. You may contact Louise about her writing, art and tours via the website www.secretlandscapetours.com.

Other Books by Roving Press

If you enjoyed this book, why not try others in our range of local titles?

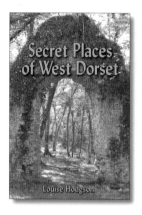

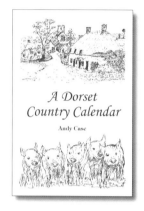

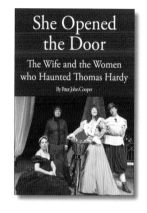

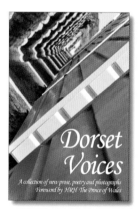

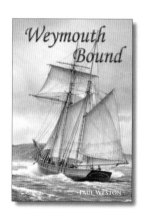

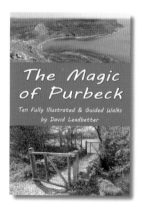

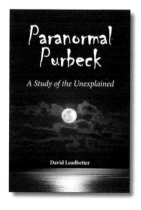

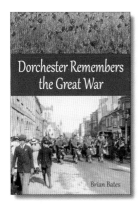

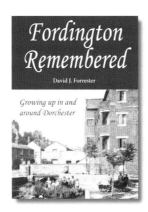

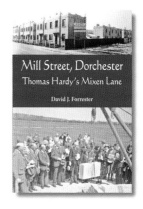

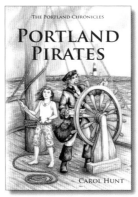

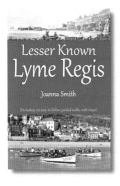

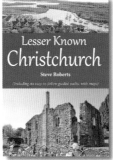

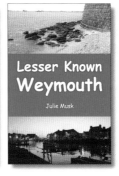

Rather like having your own personal guide, our *Lesser Known* series of books offer a close-up, contemporary view of the past and present. Quotes from local people give a unique insight, and each is packed with surprising 'lesser known' facts, stories, photographs and maps. With walks suitable for all ages, be inspired to explore and discover what many visitors, and even residents, often miss.

Roving Press

www.rovingpress.co.uk
If you like exploring, you'll love our books

Index

Cerne Abbas, gateway to the burial ground.